ROUTLEDGE LIBRARY EDITIONS:
THE HISTORY OF
ECONOMIC THOUGHT

Volume 12

AGENDA FOR A FREE SOCIETY

AGENDA FOR A FREE SOCIETY

Essays on Hayek's *The Constitution of Liberty*

Edited by
ARTHUR SELDON

Routledge
Taylor & Francis Group
LONDON AND NEW YORK

First published in 1961 by Hutchinson & Co. (Publishers) Ltd

This edition first published in 2017
by Routledge
2 Park Square, Milton Park, Abingdon, Oxon OX14 4RN

and by Routledge
711 Third Avenue, New York, NY 10017

Routledge is an imprint of the Taylor & Francis Group, an informa business

British Library Cataloguing in Publication Data
A catalogue record for this book is available from the British Library

ISBN: 978-1-138-29250-5 (Set)
ISBN: 978-1-315-23288-1 (Set) (ebk)
ISBN: 978-1-138-23843-5 (Volume 12) (hbk)
ISBN: 978-1-315-29753-8 (Volume 12) (ebk)

Publisher's Note
The publisher has gone to great lengths to ensure the quality of this reprint but points out that some imperfections in the original copies may be apparent.

Disclaimer
The publisher has made every effort to trace copyright holders and would welcome correspondence from those they have been unable to trace.

Agenda For A Free Society

Essays on Hayek's *The Constitution of Liberty*

H. B. Acton
Frederic Benham
Michael P. Fogarty
Graham Hutton
John A. Lincoln
E. Victor Morgan
E. F. Nash
A. A. Shenfield
Sir Henry Slesser
J. W. N. Watkins

Edited by Arthur Seldon

Published for
THE INSTITUTE OF ECONOMIC AFFAIRS
by
HUTCHINSON OF LONDON

HUTCHINSON & CO. (*Publishers*) LTD
178–202 Great Portland Street, London, W.1

London Melbourne Sydney
Auckland Bombay Toronto
Johannesburg New York

★

First published 1961

This book has been set in Times type face. It has been printed in Great Britain on Antique Wove paper by Taylor Garnett Evans & Co. Ltd, Watford, Herts, and bound by them

Contents

INTRODUCTION 7 *The Editor*

PART ONE: PRINCIPLES OF A FREE SOCIETY

I THE INDIVIDUAL AND SOCIETY *Graham Hutton*
The beginnings of society – Social rights and obligations – The needs and nature of community – The individual in family and community – The urge to individuality – The urgency of liberty 17

II PHILOSOPHY *J. W. N. Watkins*
Introduction – Hayek's unconservatism – Social spontaneity and the rule of law – Freedom and non-discrimination under the rule of law – Coercion and liberty – Responsibility – The justification of freedom 31

III LAW *A. A. Shenfield*
The Hayekian analysis – The nature of law – Predictability and impartiality of law – Administrative powers and administrative law – Constitutionalism and federalism – State economic action – The problem of monopoly 51

IV OBJECTIVES *H. B. Acton*
The good society – Aims of policy – The conditions of freedom – The role of independence – Freedom, knowledge and ignorance – Progress – Distributive justice – Conclusion 69

PART TWO: POLICY IN A FREE SOCIETY

V THE MONETARY FRAMEWORK *E. Victor Morgan*
Introduction – Objectives of monetary policy – The causes of inflation – The instruments of monetary policy – Rule and discretion in monetary policy – The central bank and the government – Conclusion 87

VI TAXATION — *Frederic Benham*
Progressive taxation – Minimum aggregate sacrifice – Hayek's conclusions – The British tax system – Surtax – Estate duty – A tax on personal wealth – Other possible changes 101

VII SOCIAL WELFARE — *Michael P. Fogarty*
The present state of the debate – Professor Hayek's argument – State monopoly – The alternative to state monopoly – The range of services – Non-state services – Administration of non-state services 119

VIII TRADE UNIONS AND THE LABOUR MARKET:

PART I. THE LEGAL STATUS OF TRADE UNIONS — *Sir Henry Slesser*
Origins of trade union laws – The growth and use of picketing – The 1871 Act – The 1906 Act – The status of a trade union – The Osborne judgment – The General Strike and the 1927 Act – Conflicting liberties 139

PART II. HUMAN RIGHTS IN INDUSTRY — *John A. Lincoln*
Privilege – Human rights – Rules and rights – Effects on general rights, trade union practice and law – Trade unions and the non-member – Rights and responsibilities 155

IX AGRICULTURE — *E. F. Nash*
The exceptional case? – The basic economic problem – The error of the protectionist solution – The terms of trade argument – The balance of payments argument – Costs and efficiency in protected agriculture – A way to restore free markets 171

INDEX 190

Introduction

'As a cautionary voice', said the former Marxist philosopher, Professor Sidney Hook, in his review* of *The Constitution of Liberty*, 'Mr. Hayek is always worth listening to. He is an intellectual tonic. But in our time of troubles, his economic philosophy points the road to disaster.'

A thinker who can earn praise and condemnation in such proximity and from such a committed critic must command attention. What sort of book is *The Constitution of Liberty*?† Its wide sweep takes in economics, political theory, philosophy, sociology, anthropology and jurisprudence. Its profound scholarship, drawing on or appraising more than a thousand authors, yields an intellectual feast and *tour de force*. Its modesty, humility and humanity inspire respect for a writer whose transparent aim, whatever his judgments, is solely to serve mankind. Its fearless integrity leads him to follow through his analysis to unpopular and seemingly extravagant conclusions. Not least, its aim, 'a comprehensive restatement of the basic principles of a philosophy of freedom' (p. 3) makes it a work that will live as a landmark in the history of political economy. Like Lord Robbins's work on the English classical economists, ‡ it takes us back to the masters of the eighteenth and nineteenth centuries, not least to Hayek's mentors, David Hume, Adam Smith, Edmund Burke, Lord Acton, Alexis de Tocqueville, whom we are too apt to judge secondhand from writers who have misinterpreted them. It would

* *The New York Times* Book Review, 21st February, 1960.
† Routledge & Kegan Paul, 1960.
‡ *The Theory of Economic Policy*, Macmillan, 1952.

be folly to try to assess the influence that *The Constitution of Liberty* may wield on thinkers and men of affairs in the second half of the twentieth century; yet it is safe to compare it in conception, intellectual insight and execution with Adam Smith's *Wealth of Nations*.

When philosophic terms are losing or changing their meaning, when established political party attitudes are being fused or becoming irrelevant, and when rapid social and economic change is enforcing elemental rethinking of policies, opinions and faiths, it is timely that such a writer should redefine the nature of liberty, analyse the legal and institutional framework in which it can best thrive, and review the public policies designed to preserve and extend it.

When there has been too little love of liberty on the Left and too much embracing of expediency on the Right, when socialists have become conservative and conservatives socialist, when liberals stand for the market economy on the Continent, the directed economy in North America and for versions of both in Britain, it is refreshing and thought-provoking to have it argued that lovers of liberty are none of these things but Whigs. After *The Constitution of Liberty*, no self-respecting or sensitive conservative, liberal or socialist inside or outside party will go on repeating outworn recipes or formulae with impunity.

Perhaps it was too much to expect the early reception of the book to comprise more than instinctive reactions. The newspaper and periodical notices were mostly either the uncritical appraisals of admirers or the prejudiced assaults of opponents. Later reviews have been more reflective, more balanced and more worthy assessments, but there was still need for a detailed and reasoned evaluation of the various sections of the book. Although Professor Hayek says it 'is meant to help understanding, not to fire enthusiasm' (p. 6), it has not unnaturally aroused deep emotions and provoked polemics. The Institute was interested rather in seeing what in the book was useful to thought and society and applying it to present-day Britain. It therefore conceived a symposium by specialists in the several sciences who, while preserving objectivity in judgment and freedom to criticise adversely, would yet approach *The Constitution of Liberty* with sufficient sympathy and patience to discover the significance of what it was saying, consider where it was valid or enlightening, and discuss how it could be translated into public policy. Hence the title of our book: 'Agenda' was borrowed from Jeremy Bentham who used it to mean the content of governmental action.*

Lord Robbins said in his review article in *Economica*,† which was more critical than his earlier writings might have led us to expect from one of the leading British liberal economists, that 'it may be said to be a test, not of its quality but of its readers, that even where it arouses most disagreement at least it should command respect'. Readers of this collection of essays will find that most of the authors differ from Hayek, sometimes sharply, on many issues. But they have all tried to extract what is pertinent and useful. In Part I, Graham Hutton, an economist who is also trained in the origins and nature of organised society, sets the stage. Two philosophers, Mr. Watkins and Professor Acton, discuss Hayek's philosophy and social objectives, and Mr. Shenfield, an economist and lawyer, examines the central argument that the constitution of liberty must rest on the rule of the law.

In Part II, four economists, a distinguished jurist and a sociologist examine aspects of public policy that are of outstanding contemporary importance. Professor Morgan appraises Hayek on the monetary framework of a free society and concludes, *inter alia*, in favour of a limit to the note issue. Professor Benham discusses the impact of taxation on incentives with special reference to the role of the progressive principle, and draws some forthright conclusions for British taxes. Sir Henry Slesser, in explaining how the legal powers of the trade unions have grown in the last century, concludes it is arguable that they should be reconsidered; and Mr. Lincoln, who knows the friendly society movement well, discusses the rights and duties that trade unions, their members and non-members should have. Professor Nash reviews agricultural policy and considers how free markets can be restored. Professor Fogarty writes on the welfare services and on how private provision is replacing them. Each of our authors, by quoting Hayek directly or indirectly, will make readers want to refer to the text of *The Constitution of Liberty*.‡

A central criticism of Hayek, made by several reviewers including

* *Manual of Political Economy*. Bentham also used 'non-agenda' to indicate governmental inaction. The classical economists were more alive than we are to the benefits of abstinence by governments.

† 'Hayek on Liberty', February 1961.

‡ We are indebted to the publishers, Routledge & Kegan Paul, for their agreement to this project and to authorising quotations from the book.

Lord Robbins and not discussed fully in this symposium, relates to his argument that the suppression of free markets by *dirigisme* leads inevitably to totalitarianism. Professor Henry C. Wallich, the distinguished American economist, for example, has replied that countries with a democratic tradition, such as Britain, Sweden, Norway and Australia, can tolerate centralised economic planning and retain democracy and freedom.* Yet several doubts warn against complacency. The first is that in the perspective of history, none of Wallich's countries has had planning for very long. Secondly, it is a hope based on circular reasoning to say that democratic traditions will not permit planning to go so far that it overwhelms democratic traditions. Thirdly, it may be that Hayek is trying to prove too much; his case would seem to be made even if he shows only that the risks for freedom are much larger in the directed economy.† It is for those who urge *dirigisme* to show that it does not sacrifice liberty or that its product – faster economic growth? – is worth the sacrifice. As Mr. Shenfield argues, though the danger may be remote, the warning is salutary: even if the cliff edge is some way off it is sobering to know where the slope begins.

Thus, in Britain, public preference after experience of centralised siege economy during and after the war has changed in favour of free markets. Even so, after ten years of decontrol, one employee in six is in the direct pay of central or local government, nationalised industry or semi-public corporation; more than one pound in three of income is withdrawn from private into public spending; nine out of ten children are educated in state institutions; and everyone receives, or qualifies for, social benefits. The influence of authority is accordingly extensive, and in some sectors pervasive; and the dangers cannot cavalierly be brushed aside. In such conditions of political and public patronage, can objectivity in judgment of public policy, the quality of public life, standards of moral conduct, not least the natural urge to independence, remain untouched? The bureaucrat may still, on paper, be a public servant; but, at least according to a former inspector of taxes, he is being made a public prosecutor.‡ When taxation and legal control go beyond what the citizen feels proper, he pits himself against the state and no longer

* *The Cost of Freedom*, Harper & Bros., 1960, p. 54.

† Wallich appears to accept this: 'The centralised economy puts a strain upon democracy and freedom; the free economy does not.' Op. cit., p. 57.

‡ James Coffield, *The Tax Gatherers*, Hutchinson, 1960.

regards evasion of law or tax as reprehensible, anti-social conduct. Britons may never be slaves, but, it is argued, they are being made petty criminals and wards of the state.*

But if Hayek's analysis of the dangers for freedom are not easily disposed of there is an element of inconsistency in his analysis. He rejects 'the most fatuous of all fashionable arguments' that clocks cannot be turned back because 'it expresses the fatalistic belief that we cannot learn from our mistakes, the most abject admission that we are incapable of using our intelligence' (p. 284). Yet he concludes his discussion of social welfare:

> 'It must seem doubtful . . . whether once [the monopolistic institutions of the welfare state apparatus] have been created it will ever be politically possible to get rid of them' (p. 304).

In Britain, good sense and common humanity are at last enforcing a reconsideration of the nature, extent and role of the social services. Some that are only fifty years old have already outlived their day; opinion is beginning to move and it may not be long before it becomes politically possible to reorientate the weight of social expenditure on the dwindling proportion of old people and others in need, and to redirect social activity to newer services that cannot be supplied easily through the market.

Those who urge the claims of the free market as the centrepiece of the free society have too rarely faced the need to ensure that it is understood and accepted if it is to work effectively and without social disturbance. To create and maintain the market institutions that will make industry responsive to changing techniques and demands requires something more than technical and legal expertise. The risks and sanctions of the market process must receive the moral allegiance of the people. The market must be seen not only as

* Russell Braddon, an Australian observer of the English social scene, has formed a disturbing impression of the effect on the British character of state welfare:

> '. . . today Englishmen have sacrificed much of their past and splendid defiance, and they have sacrificed it to an idol of the Welfare State, and on this idol are engraved the wholly un-English words: "The Government knows best and will tell you what to do; and what it has not time to tell you, the municipal council and the trade unions will tell you." And this, mark you, in exactly the same Britain that King Philip II of Spain could not tell; that Emperor Napoleon could not tell; that Bismarck, that Mother Russia and Kaiser Wilhelm could not tell; that Führer Adolf Hitler himself could not tell. For almost 900 years since 1066 no-one could tell you what to do; now it seems, at last, you can be told . . .' (*The Listener*, 16th February, 1961).

efficient but as good and satisfying whatever canons of justice are regarded as proper. Faith in the free economy was severely strained in the 1930's when cyclical and secular changes in international demand and supply (intensified by governmental restrictionism) threatened ruin for many employers and near-starvation for their employees. In such conditions men must be expected to associate in defence of their immediate interests as producers, even at the expense of their long-run interests as consumers. At best, this will slow down the working of the market; at worst it will disrupt it.

Some have said that the worst enemies of capitalism are the capitalists, and it often seems that the worst enemies of rising living standards for workers in general are trade unions representing sections of the most highly paid. There is still too little understanding of the principles by which Western man has chosen to live and too little readiness to 'play the game' according to the rules. This understanding and this readiness need to be heightened, and the task is largely an essay in the simplification and demonstration of great principles. It must be persuasive if the institutions Western man has nurtured to support his political systems – private property, the free market, competition – are to survive.

Is one of these institutions discretionary intervention in order to avoid or minimise the disruptive effects of social change, such as that for which Lord Robbins argued some years ago?* Some form of compensation, although formally contrary to free market principles, may be tactically advisable or unavoidable in circumstances such as those envisaged by Professor W. H. Hutt;† Professor Nash considers a special case in this volume.

Certainly, the economic, social and political requirements of market institutions require further study. Hayek does not argue for *laissez faire* but for a framework within which men may spontaneously enter into mutually advantageous relations. He will, no doubt, be thought by some liberals to be taking too many risks with power. Distrust in government is healthy; in Britain the performance even of governments that in principle have believed in limited government does not inspire confidence that they are sufficiently free

* In one of the 1954 Brookings lectures, published in *Economics and Public Policy*, Faber & Faber.

† *Economists and the Public*, 1936, and *Plan for Reconstruction*, 1940. In the latter, Hutt attempted a detailed blueprint of a systematic scheme of compensation.

from the pressures of interest or expediency to serve the common good. But organised society must run the risk of bad or indifferent government. The question is 'Which kind?' For many years in Britain and elsewhere economists and other social scientists have tried to design institutions for centralised economic direction by the state and its organs. In time they may perhaps evolve arrangements that avoid the defects displayed in their constructions so far. But if we are to make an informed choice between the two systems of society there is also need for economists to keep up to date and refine their study of the institutions of a market economy. This is what some of the authors in this book have done. The Institute thus presents it both as a critique of Hayek's *magnum opus* and more generally of what we can learn from it in understanding and managing our economic affairs in Britain; and in the latter sense it emerges as a body of practical prescriptions for governmental policy on money, taxation, welfare, labour and agriculture.

The essays were written mostly in January or February. In those of Professors Benham and Morgan there are some perceptive anticipations of changes made in the 1961 Budget.

This volume owes much to my colleague, Ralph Harris, the General Director of the Institute, whose suggestions and promptings helped to shape it. I am also grateful to the authors for their punctuality in supplying the essays and dealing with queries, and to Hutchinsons for undertaking to publish five months after delivery of the manuscripts.

April 1961 A. S.

PART ONE

Principles of a Free Society

GRAHAM HUTTON

Born in 1904 in Hertfordshire. Was educated at 'every kind of school' – state, grammar, private and public – and at London, French and German universities. After a first in economics, he was called to the Bar, taught at the London School of Economics, and in 1933 joined *The Economist*. During the war he served in the Foreign Office and the Ministry of Information. In 1948 he started business as an independent economic consultant, but continued writing, broadcasting, and serving on the boards of several companies. The best-known of his books is a study of productivity *We Too Can Prosper* (1953). A Councillor of the Royal Institute of International Affairs, and a Trustee of the Institute of Economic Affairs. He is married, has three daughters, lives in London and pursues 'the irreconcilable hobbies' of astronomy, ecclesiology, music, photography, and collecting books and early English drawings.

I

The Individual and Society

GRAHAM HUTTON

CONFLICTS between the claims of individual human beings and the societies to which they belong are as old as the human race. It is therefore surprising that few modern students of the so-called social sciences go back to first beginnings. Partly it may be that our romantic, irrational, emotional age does not want to seem like that of the great rationalists in the Enlightenment, who insisted on going back to 'the noble savage'. More probably it is because our age – despite its apparent sophistication – feels confused amid so much conflicting scientific evidence about primitive human societies from archaeologists, anthropologists, ethnologists, and others. Whatever the reasons, any contemporary treatise on political 'science', social psychology, sociology and other social disciplines is likely to eschew incursions into primitive human society and citizenship.

Professor Hayek's *magnum opus* is not concerned with our social and individual beginnings; but it is perhaps worth while first to look at what we know of the circumstances of early human society, its governance, governors and governed, before broaching the real subject of this chapter, and then coming to grips with Hayek's contribution to thought.

The beginnings of society

Little has emerged to impugn the Classical economists' hypothesis that in such early human society life was brutish, poor and short, even if it was not (to its members) nasty or solitary. The Golden Rule of charity, mercy to the weak, care for the aged and ailing, social provision for the needy, is modern and almost wholly

Christian. 'Nature red in tooth and claw' ruled the earliest human roosts of which we know anything. Nothing left by our earliest ancestors – in Africa, China, Siberia, or the caves that sheltered men of varying breeds during the Ice Age – leads us to any other conclusion than that the rule of the strong (or the erstwhile strong, sanctified in their old age by custom) prevailed over the weaker brethren, the women, and the young. That there was religion, of a magical sort, we know; and we can surmise there were priests, privileged after their wont. That there were wonderful artists we know. That there was private property we can establish at early dates; for clothing and private hoards of tools, components, etc., belonging to craftsmen, appear in hiding-places as far apart as Northern Australia, Northern Asia, Africa and Western Europe. That there were mighty hunters we know; and to believe that some primitive communism dictated 'fair shares' of a slaughtered mammoth strains credulity, in the light of the artifacts, works of art, and other material evidence coming down to us from caves, tombs and other receptacles of remote antiquity, which indicate personal possessions and even hoards.

Indeed, evidences of inequality, hierarchy and functionalism in primitive societies meet us at every turn. We know more about all this, in fact, than about the primitive human family and how it was organised. We do not even know enough yet to declare whether the monogamous gorilla-like family was typical of primitive human society. We are still extraordinarily ignorant about our antecedents. But the more we know of them, the less does it appear that there was much consultation, representation, or other aspects of modern democracy – save only, perhaps, among the *élite* of leaders. Whether in the family (in the modern, narrow, western sense), the 'extended family', or the tribal or other grouping, primitive society was authoritarian; and the movement of modern history has been away from it. This century it has been reversed.

But movements of history are never even. They are irregular, like those of cultures and civilisations. However we define human progress, what there has been has come in fits and starts: 'Far back through creeks and inlets making', and often in improbable circumstances – for example, the origin and growth of Christianity and its social ethic. Progress in social matters, like organised care of the aged and ailing, has often come during times of decadence or 'overboiling', like Baroque ages, as in ancient Egypt or Greece, the late Roman Empire and Dark Ages of Europe, in late Saxon but not so much in Norman or Renaissance England, and in late and decadent (but not early) pre-Columbian civilisations. Social conscience often comes with – rarely before – prosperity. Before that, individual or family consciences must do the work, or the weak must go to the wall.

Not the least valuable service rendered by Hayek's *Constitution of Liberty* is to remind us how recent, hard-won, and vital to human development is the widest version of personal liberty. It is important today to keep reminding oneself that the so-called welfare state and affluent society are human agglomerations, tightly organised, at the end of a run of western, Christian, or rationalist civilisations, strongly tinged with nationalism, within a unitary culture the development of which lasted at least 1,500 years. In that time, the *individual* became the measure of society. On this showing, its versions in North America belong to Western Europe and the Mediterranean, not to pre-Columbian Peru or Mexico; as, indeed, modern Peruvian and Mexican society, so rapidly becoming urban and industrial, belongs increasingly to Europe (or, as some would say, *Hispanidad*) and decreasingly to ancient Indian roots.

As Vico noted two centuries ago, and J. B. Bury reminded us two generations ago, 'the idea of progress' (the title of Bury's book) may appeal (or not) to human beings at varying times and places; but the *fact* thereof does not come about easily, evenly and equitably. Social progress can be defined as organised, institutional, voluntary or compulsory concern for the material and mental wellbeing of the group's members, and for the fullest development of their individual potentialities. It has always been a chancy affair, coming about in fits and starts, under all religions and none, in comparative austerity as well as affluence, and depending very much on the ruling *mores* of the society as they themselves have come to be as they are.

Ideas of social rights and obligations, ideas of a cohering society (to be fused out of an amorphous amalgam), ideas of the rule of law or of central or local authority – these are late comers on the human scene. They must be appreciated for what they are today: very late comers, often from foreign fields, often ill-founded, often ill-suited to their new habitat. Not all progressive human institutions have 'grown with the people'. Not all of them throw their roots deep.

That is what we should have learned by now in our 'time of troubles', and to our cost. It is therefore worth examining from an historical, sociological viewpoint the ideas of social rights and obligations in modern, urban, industrial society. That society is very late, very new, and as yet too ill-formed for downright judgments about its own nature and that of its members.

Hayek's *Constitution of Liberty* was conceived in such a modest, humble attitude towards human individuals and societies. Its treatment of such developed social institutions as the state itself, money, material (and socially-dispensed or state) welfare, town planning, trade unions, the rule of law, etc., are not inspired by some revelation from on high about the inevitability of human progress, or of some materialistic dialectic, or of some 'unfolding' of classes, classlessness, or other social institutions. Its point of departure is the human atom, the individual citizen, born willy-nilly into an inherited society which, by reason and association, he can help to change. For Hayek, he and his liberties and his degree of personal development are the measure of his state and his society, not the state a measure of him.

Social rights and obligations

The Benthamite social principle of the greatest advantage (material or immaterial) to the greatest number in the particular society has never been 'proved'. It was never susceptible of proof, though it has too often been treated as if it were. It is not necessarily the most practical counsel for statecraft. It is certainly not synonymous with democracy, as Professor Hayek shows. It is not the rule among primitive societies, and it is of very recent development. It does nothing to solve the real problem of government and justice, which is whom and how to empower as a small minority of governors. In our century it has been invoked to justify the most inhuman treatment of minorities, both within societies and as between whole nations.*

The tyranny of the majority evoked the withering contempt of all the clearest minds of the nineteenth century: De Tocqueville, John Stuart Mill, Spencer, Matthew Arnold, the Stephens; as it did nearly two millennia ago of Plato, Aristotle, and the leading Greek and

* On all this see Lord Robbins's review of *The Constitution of Liberty* in *Economica*, February 1961.

Roman statesmen. It is scarcely surprising that, in our grimmer century, when majorities trample on and even annihilate minorities, the tyranny of majorities should draw down on it Hayek's contempt: a contempt as great as that for the more common tyranny – also prevalent today – that of the minority. Hardly an intellect worth the name throughout western civilisation these two millennia past – despite all their vicissitudes of human governance, culture and belief – has dared propound and defend the social principle that whatever a temporary majority of citizens wants, (*a*) they ought to be given by their governors, and (b) the governors should always accept as a mandate for governance and justice, to the exclusion or suppression of minorities' wants or interests. The more striking is it, therefore, that in our century alone the term democracy has so widely come to be identified with so anti-social and so perilous a principle. Nascent nations in other continents than Europe have pleaded in aid this dangerous principle as if it had been sanctified – instead of disgraced – by the most delinquent of all European political and social systems: those of Nazi Germany, Stalinist Russia, and Fascist Italy. It is the great merit of Hayek's book that it forces us back to this among other first principles of social life, at a time in our world's affairs when these have so widely been forgot or abjured.

Secondly, the movement of western history and progress – let all 'progressives' note it well – has been *away from* the principle that each individual citizen exists for the greater glory of the society. It has been *towards* the principle that society and its institutions exist, and should be varied and organised, for the greater development of each individual citizen's potentialities. Nor has it only been towards the notion that society and its institutions exist, at any one point in time, mainly or merely for the development of the *majority* of citizens' potentialities, or to gratify only their wants and not those of minorities. As societies become affluent, many collective, compulsory provisions for minimum elements in a standard of life become unnecessary. Social adaptability demands individualism and differentiation.

From this historical viewpoint, our century, as outlined in the preceding paragraph, has been a backward-falling stage in a long social process, simply because it has raised 'government by majority' to an overriding pitch of unreality, crassness and standardising banality. It has confused minority with majority, tyranny with 'people's democracy', oligarchy with (literally) mon-archy. What was Stalin's system? What is Mr. Khrushchev's? What, indeed, is the American or British or Ghanaian or South African system today? Individual needs are repressed, individual initiative constricted. (Modern technology is at least helping to save us all, by imposing in the field of education the imperative social need to find and train new *élites*: witness the political travail currently disturbing American, Russian and British society.) The clamant need for selective education, and more unequal rewards for unequal contributions to society, needs of leadership in so many fields, flat banality in the arts (especially the new mass-consumed arts) – these contemporary features of both western and non-western (but industrialising, urbanising) society evoke heart-searchings in all old, traditional political and social groupings: witness the travail now troubling both communist and socialist movements, trade unions, and other collectivist organisations. One could almost say that western mankind, and a lot more, have been turned liberal or whig or individualistic by the unfolding of terrible collectivist realities, coupled with a peep or two at the mechanistic, materialistic future.

Hayek adumbrates, ahead of his time, many problems of society and individuals which can be said to develop 'beyond the welfare state'. 'The wave of the future' today is emphatically not bearing forward a blind, monolithic, individual-crushing juggernaut of collectivism. On the contrary, in Russia as elsewhere it bears forward new, humble, tentative, worried social experiments for the eliciting and encouragement of outstanding individuals, leaders and experts. Of course one social era does not neatly dovetail into another; there is overlap; and one does not expect to hear (though one has recently heard) dogmas, myths and slogans gainsaid by their erstwhile criers overnight. But in the last five years the leading western industrial societies – including Russia and Japan – seem to have been hewing back to the old lines of historical movement, away from a blanketing collectivism and towards greater selectivity of (and respect for) individual citizens, as compared with their state of mind in 1945 or 1950. Hayek reverts to this encouraging – because individual-respecting – trend again and again. He was one of the first to spot the disillusion with the Left (see pp. 253–7). It is a most hopeful sign. Any grouping or government deliberately trying to counter that movement will be running the serious risk of missing the great tides of the world: of being swept into a backwater of history.

The needs and nature of community

Thirdly, since human societies – as we have hitherto known them – are now in the melting-pot, and no one knows whether even China will be integral and unitary in governance or defence a decade from now, we may well ask what *any* society is for. There was a time, within memory, when such a question could easily be answered. It is getting harder to answer every year: or, perhaps to put it better, it is getting harder to envisage *the* new and ultimate form of human society. The finest minds among the Americans, British, and Russians already know that their own traditional societies cannot much longer be run as they have been until now: economically, or for defence, or in terms of political systems, or dispensation of justice, or even in terms of the new powers and mobilities of the citizenry. (The Russians cannot – though they could a generation ago – *keep* industrial or agricultural workers employed in given places; the vast needs of manpower for police and military would break the economic system down.) If, therefore, the needs and nature of society itself are changing so fast, mainly for technological reasons, is it not old-fashioned, out-of-date, for politicians or other groupings to invoke, think of, or talk about 'the need to subordinate the claims of the citizen to those of society'? *What* claims of *what* new society? This is old-fashioned, nation-state, pre-technological ideology, with its dogmas, myths and shibboleths.

Can any mind, hoping to keep up with our times, really lay down that old-line socialist or communist – or, for that matter, the old-line private-enterprise individualist – institutions and organisation of society are most likely to provide what the society and citizens of the very near future will need? Already in education alone the experts of Russia, America and Britain are in a welter of disputation: 'all-round' or specialist, a bit of both, or a new ruling *élite* of narrowed experts? No wonder the (contemporary) governors of Russia are as concerned as those of Britain or the United States. How much more acute does the social problem become when one takes, instead, the organisation of politics and government itself in the new society, or the rule of law, or the reconciliation of the economic (and social) interests of the fast-multiplying groups of technicians and experts by government and by employers (whether state or private)! In the light of our technical advances, the old query 'What is society for?' acquires new sense.

Our interdependence is not diminishing – either inside our nations or between them – it is increasing fast: in economics, in defence, even in government itself (for national units are, with increasing obviousness, becoming too small for efficiency and for defence; hence the burgeoning groupings of nations). Even persons now move, under their own mechanical motive power, from country to country. Mobility has become a prized personal right; and soon now the ordinary citizen-householder will not even be dependent upon local services of heat, light, power, etc., all of which will be as immediately generated by the citizen as he (or she) is mobile. Only the home, it may be assumed, will remain 'on location', with its attendant sanitary, marketing, educational, and other amenities. Thus our techniques make nations too small, but their citizens too big and mobile. The only possible reconciliation of all this with the claims of government, justice, etc., is a dual process: federation or confederation of the big units at the top (the international aspect), and administrative devolution at the lower levels (the national aspect). It hardly needs to be emphasised that all this is far from the pristine early twentieth-century ideas of all-absorbing, centralising collectivism.

By the same token, the individual citizen – if only he is educated enough to know what he needs, and to want it – stands to carve out for himself and his family, or local community, a wider field for self-realisation and for the development of all his potentialities in a society so altered. At the same time the internationalisation of so many problems, formerly nationally solved, presents the old-fashioned, centralised, monolithic, nationalistic collectivism with formidable and unimagined conundrums. (The *Dogmenstreit* between China and Russia, with Albania, Jugoslavia, Poland and others on the sidelines, is only an adumbration of what we may yet expect to see, as African and Asian sovereignties multiply and nationalistic versions of collectivisms become variegated.) All this is far from the simple, authoritarian, theocratic states of ancient Egypt or Mexico or Peru, where the individual could safely be ignored or sacrificed for the greater glory of the state or the gods, or both. At least in one respect the citizen of a modern, western, industrial state may draw encouragement from contemporary trends: it may not be long before it will be harder for his state to survive than for him and his family. These, too, are aspects of society 'beyond the welfare state', and *The Constitution of Liberty* throws revealing light on them in many places.

The individual in family and community

Fourthly, however, we have also during our century strayed from the basic and elemental social concepts of community: the individual as a member first of his family, and then of the local community in which that family lives. The 'welfare state' has indubitably weakened, not strengthened, family ties. Partly of course the increased personal mobility, coupled with the rapid change in morals and ethics, has broken down these primeval, communal cells. Just as the original inspiration and *raisons d'être* of socialism and trade unions have disappeared, leaving in their place contemporary power or party and much dogma and doctrine *minus* intellectual content, so village and city, town and suburb, parents and adolescent children and grandparents have all found themselves 'out of place and infinitely irrelevant' in our new, technically necessary, settings. Our nations and their lay-out, our landscapes, our socially inherited attitudes and implied loyalties, our very highway and rail and canal connections – these come to us from other ages, other sets of values. They are all undergoing change, sometimes rudely. But under all these challenged surfaces lie deep human needs, keen emotions, complex sentiments; and while we change our landscape, communications, habits, attitudes, ways of living, we must remain aware that our deeper human needs and feelings remain and must be assuaged.

The countryman is now mobile and does not apparently need the village to which he 'belongs'; but he needs continuing human companionship and seeks it elsewhere. The adolescent matures earlier and does not apparently need parents; he (or she) seeks group life elsewhere than in the home. The industrial city dweller seeks the green rim of the countryside for his home; he does not apparently need the civic amenities of the great centre, nor does he or his wife go inwards to that centre any more than is necessary. Yet all of these people – individual citizens following their free fancies – could not indulge their fancies, or subsist long, or remain normal adjusted human beings capable of fully developing their potential faculties, without the complex, unobserved, even international, but beautifully dovetailed services of a vast and invisible organism of fellow-men. The countryman dashes to the town; the townsman to the country; the adolescent shuns his parents, but drops the responsibility on to teachers, companions, or employers. There is no way of developing the individual's potentialities to the full, other than in *some* grouping of society.

Where we have so often erred this grim century is in thinking that 'the state' or 'the government' or 'the authorities' should naturally step in to do everything we no longer wanted family, parents, local community, or even ourselves alone to do. There is no reason, there is only a lazy nonchalance, which makes the state so all-powerful in the citizens' private affairs today. It is a dangerous nonchalance which leaves so much of the private sector for the public sector to control, since 'the public sector' at any one moment is only what a few people temporarily in power say, or leave to underlings to say, to the citizen. There is no civic virtue or principle in such negligence, which empowers authorities to control so much of personal lives. Nor is there any of the former, elementally satisfying, communal life. Hence the universal hatred – it is shared in Russia, where it is caricatured – of bureaucracy, petty Bumbledom, and *paperasserie:* the domain of Parkinson's Law. Indeed, so much has been put upon the shoulders of civil servants and state functionaries, which would better have been performed by private citizens, that one can almost sympathise with these public servants if they think that the public was created for them to administer.

Family and community life have certainly suffered grievously in the last two generations; probably more in Asia and Africa even than in the West. But that is only another way of saying that our societies have developed too fast from the stage at which family and community life *was* satisfactory; that, therefore, to make them satisfactory to their members again means developing, consciously, both family and community life to suit the changed and changing social settings. We can never put our entire societies back. Yet if we do not contrive to reintroduce the deeper emotional satisfactions of what we can call "petty communal life" – i.e. in family and local community – we shall certainly fail to get in our widening societies (still more so in federations of them) that cohering, strong, social cement that withstands all shocks and holds the individual citizens together like bricks in a well-bonded wall.

The urge to individuality

Fifth and lastly, there is another deep human proclivity – it is often a need – for social differentiation: to be different from the next chap, to be outstanding or eccentric, not to be a cog or cipher, not to have to live and think and eat and work and play exactly as one's fellows. Wise commanders of men in armed forces know this, and make provision for satisfying this urge in constructive ways – despite the proverbial sameness and discipline and anonymity of the armed services. No one likes 'to rust unburnish'd, not to shine in use'. No one likes to be classed always among the herd of anonymous poll-cattle. (Even when A/C Shaw sought anonymity in the R.A.F. from his renown as T. E. Lawrence of Arabia, he bought a very *classé* motor bicycle capable of such high speeds that it took away his life.) Super- and sub-ordination, hierarchies, *élites*, classes and even religious castes, leadership and followership, personality and lack of it, outstanding ability and lack of it, manners and graces and lack of them, education and lack of it, animal courage and lack of it, even oratory, poetry, singing and the lack of them – these things from the dawn of the human race have differentiated individuals and small groupings within the larger group called a society. Privileges have gone with those qualities: with the heroism of warriors or hunters, or with the skills of a ball game (as among the ancient Maya of Yucatán); with crude gladiators or exquisite senators; with priests (as in ancient Egypt or Mexico) and kings and thegns; with witch-doctors, magicians and other clever men; and with artificers of the first metal tools and weapons, or the first precious and fragile family pots.

No such thing as absolute equality of treatment for all adult citizens, male and female, in economic and political matters has ever been established in any known and natural human society. (It has only been artificially enforced in specially insulated, organised, communities like the Thebaid, monasteries, some sects, or cities besieged, and then not always for long.) Against so vast and universal a backcloth for human society, the pretensions of a few intellectuals in the last century or two – monumentally out of touch with the real desires of the overwhelming masses of their fellows – seem overweening. If it had not been for the limited successes of a few Christian closed communities so organised in earlier ages and poorer times, it is to be doubted whether the intellectuals advocating equality of material circumstances for all adult citizens would ever have gained as much support as they did. Once again, what has happened in our century has been aberration. In any case the trend is now the other way, and the coherence of our societies will be the greater for it (see Hayek, pp. 253–7).

The urgency of liberty

There remains one point – *the* cardinal point of Hayek's work – and the point of all social life which it is impossible, particularly today, to over-emphasise. It is that whatever one's race, colour or creed, one must admit the necessity of 'freedom' as the environment within which the ultimate social atom, the individual, develops to the fullest extent his or her potentialities. One can debate – indeed, one does, violently – in what 'this freedom' consists or ought to consist. But society cannot deny individuals (particularly when young) the dangerous right to come to almost all of their own decisions, often wrongly (as it appears by hindsight), in a setting of the greatest personal freedom possible, without at the same time laming them and society.

This or that society, this or that political or legal system, will circumscribe or enlarge 'this freedom' for the citizens according to age-limits, sex, education, or other qualifications. Societies will accordingly vary in quality, dynamics and durability. But the principle stands like a rock, unshaken by millennia of human development, under bewilderingly variegated social guises: the ultimate unit of society which feels all pleasure and all pain is the individual. The same unit appreciates all 'the glories of our blood and state' or depreciates them. The same unit makes the strength or the weakness of the body politic, the nation, the civilisation. The same unit builds – and unbuilds – cultures, and arts and crafts; advances techniques; makes all inventions and applications; respects or denigrates all values. And we must confess that, despite our awe-inspiring progress in material techniques, we are still far from knowing much about the processes whereby we can multiply favourable mutations in human germ cells, or even spread a little thicker on our societies the still dangerously thin top layer of intelligence. On the contrary, we seem this century rather to have perfected the material means for multiplying unfavourable mutations and even for thinning-down our top veneer of intelligence.

Such is the historical and contemporary backcloth against which Hayek plays out the ideas and principles of *The Constitution of Liberty*. The theme is worthy of its occasion in a 'time of troubles' and of 'the breaking of nations'. It is as if the author had looked back along the way humanity had struggled, and then had looked across the world as it is, and had managed to convey in one book the amplitude and the sublimity, the weight and the scope, of the challenge to humanity in our era. Whatever critics of the book in our era may say – and it affords grounds for constructive criticism, as does every seminal work – it will remain as much, perhaps even more, a book for the ages. For it could only have been provoked, it could only have been written, in our chaotic, desperately anxious, yet stimulating and responsive era. Such works of great minds bear fruit hereafter.

J. W. N. WATKINS

Born 1924. Educated at R.N. College, Dartmouth. Served as destroyer navigator and torpedo officer during the war. Resigned commission after the war. Graduated from the London School of Economics in 1949. Henry Fellow at Yale University 1949–50. Has been on staff of London School of Economics since 1950 and is now Reader in the History of Philosophy in the University of London. Has contributed articles to *Analysis*, *Australasian Journal of Philosophy*, *British Journal for the Philosophy of Science*, *Encounter*, *Ethics*, *Journal of Philosophy*, *Mind*, *Philosophical Quarterly*, *Philosophy*, *Philosophy of Science*, *Proceedings of the Aristotelian Society*, *Ratio*, *Rationalist Annual*, *Review of Politics*, and to several anthologies. Has delivered a number of broadcasts. Working on a book. At present (1961) Heath Visiting Professor at Grinnell College, U.S.A. Married, with four children.

II

Philosophy

J. W. N. WATKINS

Introduction

IN any circumstances *The Constitution of Liberty* would have been an important book. Given the condition of political philosophy in the English-speaking world today, it is outstandingly important. In recent years contributions to political philosophy have consisted almost exclusively either of historical work, often of a high scholarly excellence* but hardly attempting to bring the ideas discussed to bear on modern issues, or of occasional *ballons d'essai* which have not risen very high despite the absence of mooring-lines.†

Professor Hayek's book is rich in historical material, but it is not primarily historical. At the end of it, he speaks of 'the principles I have tried to reconstruct by piecing together the broken fragments of a tradition' (p. 411). His massive annotation is not a mere scholarly indulgence. It indicates much better than Hayek's own listings of his heroes (e.g. Milton, Burke, Macaulay, Gladstone, de Tocqueville, Lord Acton) the range and detail of the material he has digested and organised into a coherent and comprehensive, distinctive and uncompromising political philosophy. At the centre of this philosophy is a view of the way in which social processes of adaptation and development work and of the proper role of human deliberation and planning within them. Whereas in *The Counter-Revolution of Science* and *The Road to Serfdom* this view was pressed home against

* E.g. H. Warrender, *The Political Philosophy of Hobbes*; A. G. Wernham, ed., *Spinoza*: *The Political Works*; P. Laslett, ed., *Locke's Two Treatises of Government*.

† An exception to this generalisation is Sir Isaiah Berlin's *Two Concepts of Liberty*, which is both historically rooted and relevant to the present day.

socialist doctrines, in *The Constitution of Liberty* it is pressed home against the welter of dubious practices and expedients which inflation, progressivist slogans, pressures, ill-conceived projects, administrative convenience, and downright intellectual laziness and dishonesty have brought into existence in the post-war Western world. I have the highest admiration for the controversial chapters on trade unions, taxation, town planning, agriculture and education where the principles worked out earlier are applied with salutary and sometimes startling effect. This presents a leftish reviewer with an easy way of dismissing the book. He has only to hold up for amazed inspection some of its more drastic recommendations without mentioning the arguments behind them, and to shake his head over their shocking and unrealistic character. I think that Hayek does press his proposals with a somewhat doctrinaire insistence, and that a lighter and less insistent style would have been more effective. But what matters is not so much the book's practical conclusions as the views behind them – both of the way a society should work and of the way contemporary policies actually work. Whether or not these views are true – and I suspect that Hayek's understanding of contemporary policies is more detailed and shrewd than that of some of his critics – they certainly constitute a challenging corrective idea; and the only adequate way for a leftish critic to meet Hayek's challenge would have been to come to grips with this corrective idea, and not just to pour scorn on the proposals to which it leads.

These remarks have carried me into territory reserved for other contributors to this symposium. My concern is limited to the more distinctly philosophical aspects of his book. This limitation has its drawbacks. Part of the significance of the book lies precisely in the fact that it organises into a *system* philosophical, sociological, economic, legal, historical, and political views; and it is a pity that symposiast reviewing requires this unusual unity to be broken up. Moreover, I believe that there are certain weaknesses in his philosophical position which are of no great importance for his view of society and government, but which someone confined to philosophical matters is obliged to be finicky about.

After indicating the unconservative character of his thinking, I shall describe the two theses which run through the book and the connections between them. Then I shall turn finicky. The first point I shall discuss is whether, for Hayek, living under a rule of law *entails* being free or tends to *foster* freedom; the second is Hayek's criterion for excluding discriminatory laws which contravene his idea of a rule of law. Next, I shall examine in a fault-finding way his related definitions of 'coercion' and 'liberty'. Then I shall come down heavily on his notion of responsibility. Finally, I shall ask whether something important has not been left out of his argument for freedom.

I should have written differently had I been free to roam among all the interesting arguments in the book. Let me correct in advance any false impression my subsequent niggling may create by declaring unambiguously that this is the most important book in its field since the war.

Hayek's unconservatism

The reader should not be misled by the warmth of Hayek's admiration for Hume and Burke into supposing that Hayek's criticisms of socialist, collectivist and *dirigiste* tendencies are inspired by distrustfulness of all ideals and general theories of society. Although their targets are sometimes the same, Hayek's standpoint is quite different from, say, that of Oakeshott in his attacks on rationalist politics in the early issues of the *Cambridge Journal*. His book has a high, idealistic tone. In his Preface, Hayek states: 'My aim is to picture an *ideal*, to show how it can be achieved, and to explain what its realization would mean in practice' (p. vii, my italics); and in a Postscript entitled 'Why I am not a Conservative' he underlines his hostility to the conservative's opportunism and distrust of general principles and of novel ideas and developments, his authoritarianism and nostalgia for old ways. If Hayek defends certain 'long-established institutions' it is not because they are old but because they correspond to his ideals (p. 399). He favours piecemeal change but it should be 'guided by some general conception of the social order desired, some coherent image of the kind of world in which the people want to live' (p. 114). Sometimes his unconservative attitude displays itself in rather surprising suggestions – for instance, that the House of Commons and other assemblies which combine ministerial and legislative functions should be split into two, each with its proper function (p. 207), or that we should not accept the nation-state as the ultimate unit (p. 263) – though such suggestions are not pressed.*

* Perhaps the fact that Hayek does not condemn ideal schemes for society as such, but only schemes which would in practice be harmful and dangerous, helps to explain why John Milton, that arch-visionary, the Saint-Just of the Puritan Rebellion, figures among his heroes.

One great merit of Hayek's high-minded – if you like, his doctrinaire – approach is its explicitness. Sometimes his practical conclusions coincide with those of conservative writers. The difference is that he provides coherent and far-reaching justifications for them. Sometimes his conclusions are definitely to the right of anything a cautious conservative would dare to propose. To the objection (as likely to come from a conservative as from a progressivist) that 'we cannot turn the clock back' he makes the scathing retort:

> 'One cannot help wondering whether those who habitually use this cliché are aware that it expresses the fatalistic belief that we cannot learn from our mistakes, the most abject admission that we are incapable of using our intelligence' (p. 284).

Social spontaneity and the rule of law

Two fundamental ideas pervade the book. One is that, within a framework of law and morality, social processes should be spontaneous, the outcome of people making the best they can of their luck and capacities and resources, and not subject to monopolistic distortion or overall direction. The other is that men should be governed by general laws and not by specific orders and directions. These two ideas are closely connected. And they jointly generate the theme of the book, which is that coercion – in the sense of men being shoved around or bullied or forced to do what they do not want to do by other men – should be minimised, that men should, so far as possible, be constrained only by impersonal factors, by the laws of nature, the laws of the state, and blind social and market forces, and not by particular people and groups.

I shall first sketch his argument for freedom from the need for social spontaneity; then the connection between this and his argument for a rule of law.

Although Hayek's scheme is a sort of blue-print for a good society, it differs from many other such schemes in being so to speak, algebraical – the variables are not filled in by the author but are left to be filled in by chance and circumstance and individual initiative. It is a scheme for maximising the possibility of improving social knowledge and of employing it to better effect; but the whole point is that the actual process of improving and re-deploying social knowledge cannot be controlled. It can be planned for, but it cannot be planned. What specific advantages will accrue from the process cannot be laid down or foretold. At bottom, Hayek's economic argument for liberty is an extension to society at large of the argument for academic freedom: the more tightly research is controlled, the more it is confined within the limitations of existing expectations, the less likely becomes the discovery of unexpected results. Social life, on Hayek's view, mainly consists of individuals each making use, in his transactions, of vast amounts of knowledge of which he is largely unaware (p. 22, p. 25). This knowledge is the resultant of a great many experiments and adaptations. For the most part it is incorporated in practices, skills, institutional arrangements and technological achievements. In so far as it is articulate knowledge it is dispersed among many people. It would be impossible to centralise more than a small part of it. Just as research must be free if science is not to be frozen up, so personal initiative and resourcefulness must not be hamstrung if our social knowledge is to grow, and to be better used.

This view yields certain appraisals which, although they are mutually compatible, do not usually go together. On the one hand, Hayek has none of the conservative's dislike of rapid innovation. Social innovation is made possible by and in its turn makes possible new ideas. New problems arise, new solutions are attempted, which are instructive even if they fail. At each step, something is added to the dispersed stock of social knowledge. On the other hand, this view leads Hayek to a frank appreciation of the social utility of wealthy men, especially if they are the independent controllers of their fortunes, and to forebodings about the widening of the class of salaried managers and technicians. The latter have little inducement or opportunity for bold experimentation. The former may indulge in inedifying extravagance; but they have the means, and may have the incentive, to try out or patronise, new ideas in commerce, art, industry and social living. Without them, society would be deprived of an important source of innovation. And since innovations which later become popular and cheap usually start as the costly indulgences of rich men, a society which allows its envy of wealth to get the upper hand will deprive itself of future benefits.

I now turn to the connections between his social-spontaneity thesis and his rule-of-law thesis.

The connection is best seen if we consider *infringements* of these two theses. It would be an infringement of the social-spontaneity thesis if government officials were to single out certain private persons and order them to carry out specific actions, not because some general law requires this, but because the officials were trying to steer social processes in particular directions.

Such ordering about, though it might be perfectly legal, would likewise be a complete contravention of Hayek's admirably strict conception of a rule of law,* according to which laws should be general, their incidence predictable and conflict with them avoidable. A specific administrative order of the kind we are considering is none of these. It singles out particular people for whom its incidence is unpredictable. And unlike a prohibition which may leave an indefinite number of alternative courses of action open, it is a positive order which makes one particular course of action compulsory.

There is a second, somewhat looser, connection between Hayek's two theses: both are inspired by the idea of 'order without commands', to use one of his sub-headings. Admittedly, the meaning of 'order' is rather different in the two cases. In one the idea is that a social and economic *system* emerges from the impersonally co-ordinated activities of numerous centres of initiative, this system or 'order' being in most ways far superior, in its use of resources and capacity for change and growth, to any rival system which individual ingenuity might devise (pp. 110–1). In the other, 'order without commands' means a legal system of general rules, judicially administered, superior to government official and private citizen alike, providing a stable and predictable framework for individual activities, and within which no one is at the behest of another person, no one enjoying any discretionary legal power. (To avoid misunderstanding it should be said that, unlike some of the older liberals who believed in a pure *Rechtsstaat*, Hayek does *not* confine the state's function to the enactment and enforcement of general laws. He regards it as the state's function to provide various services which would be under-provided by other methods, especially the spreading of information; and their provision, like the provision of a service by a private body, will involve considerable administrative discretion.

* How far Hayek's position is from conservative opportunism is indicated by a quotation he gives on p. 243 from a pamphlet by Conservative lawyers which commends administrative tribunals because, 'flexible and unbound by rules of law or precedent, they can be of real assistance to their minister in carrying out policy'.

But the essential point is that it should not involve discretionary *coercion* over private people.)

A third connection between his two theses is provided by Hayek's attitude to monopoly. His belief, as an economist, is that large commercial monopolies usually arise only under the shelter of various governmental policies and that the best way to discourage them is simply not to encourage them artificially. If a company does manage to secure a quasi-monopolistic position for itself by commercial methods and without political assistance, it will usually thereby set in motion corrective tendencies. In the meanwhile, its temporary enjoyment of quasi-monopolistic status will not be so very harmful or economically distorting *provided it is required to treat all-comers alike* (p. 136). Now the state ought to have a monopoly of coercive and judicial power. This is one field where we do *not* want competition. But such a monopoly will be dangerous unless the state, like other monopolists, treats all-comers alike. Its coercive power should be used mainly to prevent coercion (p. 144). As Hayek pointed out in *The Road to Serfdom*, a desirable attribute which a competitive economy shares with an impartial legal system is that both are 'blind', i.e. no respecter of persons (p. 76).

A fourth connection between Hayek's two theses is, again, best brought out by considering infringements of them. If a government tries to take control of some social process, it will, in so far as it succeeds, create something which reflects its own conscious plans instead of using the knowledge which would have been used if the process had been allowed to develop freely within the social framework. Similarly, if a judge or an administrator were to set aside the law and trust to his own discretion in a particular case, he would be deciding to rely upon his personal knowledge and to wave aside the very considerable experience which the law incorporates. For laws are seldom created *en bloc*. With statute law, almost as much as with case law, a long process of trial and error has usually brought the law into its present shape – very many people, directly or indirectly, at one time or another, have had a say in it. Thus Hayek's belief in the uncentralisability of social knowledge implies that infringements of his anti-*dirigisme* thesis and of his rule-of-law thesis both entail that a relatively small amount of personal information is being preferred to an inter-personal stock of knowledge which is much richer, largely unstated, and widely dispersed.

Freedom and non-discrimination under the rule of law

I now turn to two difficulties I have with Hayek's rule-of-law thesis.

The first difficulty is that Hayek sometimes suggests that in a society where the rule of law prevails men will automatically, as a *logical* consequence, be free in the sense of being uncoerced by other men;* and sometimes that in such a society men are *as a matter of fact likely* to be freer than in a society where the rule of law does not prevail.†

For Hayek's purposes it is surely sufficient to say that there is a causal connection between a rule of law and personal freedom. Indeed, it defeats his purpose to say that there is a necessary connection, for a necessary connection could only be manufactured by suitable definitions of 'rule of law' and 'freedom'; and the manufacture of such a necessary connection makes it impossible to assert what Hayek really wants to assert, namely that there is a causal connection between a rule of law and freedom.

Hayek's definition of 'coercion' will be the subject of the next section. There I shall claim that that definition has been distorted by Hayek's desire to assimilate civil laws and other social conditions which impinge on people in an impersonal and indiscriminate way to natural laws and natural conditions which cannot be regarded as coercive, and that this distorted definition has several awkward consequences. Here I only want to show that it has the awkward consequence of creating a merely verbal and necessary connection between 'rule of law' and 'freedom'.

Hayek's idea is that freedom is absence of coercion and that general laws, unlike personal commands, are non-coercive because of their conditional and non-categorical character. He writes:

> 'Provided that I know beforehand that if I place myself in a particular position, I shall be coerced and provided that I can avoid putting myself in such a position, I need never be coerced. At least in so far as the rules providing for coercion are not aimed at me personally but are so framed as to apply equally to all people in similar circumstances, they are no different from any of the natural obstacles that affect my plans' (p. 142).

* 'When we obey laws, in the sense of general abstract rules laid down irrespective of their application to us, we are not subject to another man's will and are therefore free' (p. 153).

† 'It is not to be denied that even general, abstract rules, equally applicable to all, may possibly constitute severe restrictions on liberty. But when we reflect on it, we see how very unlikely this is . . .' (pp. 154–5). Hayek uses the words 'liberty' and 'freedom' interchangeably to mean absence of coercion (p. 11).

An able-bodied British male citizen in 1800 would have known that if he placed himself in Portsmouth he risked being press-ganged; but he could avoid Portsmouth, and need never be coerced by the press-gang. The press-gang was not aimed at him personally. It was no different from a natural obstacle, such as an outbreak of the plague (which also takes its victims at random) in Portsmouth, which might equally have affected his plans.

Something has gone wrong; it seems to me that Hayek has been over-impressed by the following logical consideration: a prohibition leaves an agent free to act in any of the indefinitely large number of ways compatible with not acting in the prohibited way, whereas a positive command leaves him unfree to act in any of the indefinitely large number of ways incompatible with acting in the commanded way. This seems to suggest that a prohibition is infinitely less coercive than a command. But we must not be dazzled by the largeness of the number of alternative courses left open by a prohibition. After all, the agent can select only one of them. To measure the degree of penalisation which a prohibition involves, what we have to weight against the prohibited course is not the whole class of unprohibited alternatives but just that unprohibited alternative which he dislikes least. Now it may be that his best unprohibited alternative will be little or no worse than the prohibited course, in which case he will not be penalised by the prohibition. But it may also be that he regards the best unprohibited alternative as *much* worse than the prohibited course. Suppose he is confronted by a 'general, abstract rule, equally applicable to all', which forbids foreign travel; and suppose he has an ailing father abroad whom he wants to visit before he dies. On Hayek's argument, there is no coercion or loss of freedom here. This agent is not subject to anyone's will. He is just confronted by the fact that if he tries to go abroad he will be apprehended and punished. He might equally have been confronted by the fact that he has not enough money for the trip or that the trip would take so long that his father would be dead before he arrived.

Instead of using the word 'coerced' Hayek should, I think, have written: 'Provided that I know beforehand that if I place myself in a particular position, I shall be *punished* and provided that I can avoid putting myself in such a position, I need never be *punished*.' So amended, this statement is true, but no longer supports the contention that coercion is impossible under a rule of law (for the cost of avoiding punishment may be intolerable) or even the contention that there is *less* coercion under a rule of law (for under a *dirigiste* system one could likewise avoid punishment by obeying the specific commands directed at one personally). Hayek's best argument here is that since, where the rule of law prevails, the laws apply equally to everybody, obnoxious laws and laws which severely curtail freedom are unlikely to be tolerated by those in power.

The second difficulty concerns just what it means for a law to be general, abstract and equally applicable to all, i.e. non-discriminatory and consistent with a rule of law. Hayek quotes with approval Rousseau's remark that 'anything that relates to a named individual is outside the scope of legislative authority' (p. 194); but it is well known that, given that no one individual is exactly similar to another, it is always possible in principle to pick out a particular individual, not by mentioning his name, but by providing a sufficiently specific general characterisation which fits only him. And, of course, a law can be perfectly general and abstract and yet discriminate against a certain class of men. No doubt with this in mind, Hayek adds the interesting requirement that a law, besides being general and abstract, should be equally acceptable to those it hits and those it does not. I put a tick of approval against this additional requirement when I first read it – is not the difference between, say, some law in connection with *apartheid* and, say, the law requiring third-party insurance precisely this, that the former is *not* equally acceptable to whites and non-whites whereas the latter probably is equally acceptable to motorists and non-motorists? But I became less certain of its validity when I found the use to which Hayek puts it in connection with progressive taxation. He says many interesting and persuasive things against a rising rate of taxation; but one argument I found dubious was the argument that it contravenes the rule of law since only a flat rate would be equally acceptable to rich and poor. I began to wonder whether, if the idea of general, abstract laws by itself is too weak, the idea of general, abstract laws equally acceptable to those hit and those not hit might not be too strong an interpretation of what the rule of law requires. Are laws against, say, sexual assault equally acceptable to those hit by them and those not hit? Hayek wants to provide a *definite* criterion for a rule of law, a criterion which will mean the same to people with different moral outlooks; so his criterion must not contain any moral notions. At the same time, the idea for which he is trying to provide an objective criterion is, I am confident, an essentially moral idea, namely that a general abstract law which penalises a certain class of people, impersonally characterised, conforms to the idea of a rule of law only if this penalisation is required on grounds of decency, or fairness, or some other moral ground. It is always immensely difficult to provide a list of necessary and sufficient good-making or right-making factual characteristics for some moral notion, and I do not think that Hayek has quite succeeded. But he has introduced an important new idea into the discussion; and it may be that a somewhat modified version of this idea of equal acceptability will at last make it possible to distinguish laws which conform to the idea of a rule of law from laws which do not.

Coercion and liberty

I now turn to certain difficulties in Hayek's notion of coercion. As he says, 'we provisionally defined freedom as the absence of coercion. But coercion is nearly as troublesome a concept as liberty itself' (p. 133).

Because of his desire to assimilate impersonal social forces and general civil laws to the non-coercive forces and laws of nature, Hayek, whose philosophical views are otherwise in line with the empiricist tradition, is not able to define unfreedom in the way empiricists usually have, namely as a condition where someone is hindered by external obstacles from doing what he wants to do. For one may, of course, be hindered by natural obstacles; and Hayek feels that there is an essential difference between such hindrance and hindrances wilfully put in one's way by other people. Furthermore, he feels that there is a similar difference between being hindered by man-made forces which, however, are neither the expression of one man's will nor directed at anyone in particular, and a particular person being controlled by another. Thus his desiderata require that a definition of unfreedom should not be *merely* in terms of external obstacles but in terms of external constraints of a special kind, namely those due to personal control by some people over other people.

I have already argued that Hayek's definition of 'freedom' is *too wide*: it covers conditions (such as that of our imaginary citizen prevented by law from visiting his dying father) which most people would not regard as conditions of freedom. Now it can happen that a definition which is too wide is also too narrow.* I shall argue that this is the case with Hayek's definition of freedom.

Hayek's initial definition of 'coercion' – 'freedom' being defined as the absence of coercion – is this: 'Coercion occurs when one man's actions are made to serve another man's will, not for his own but for the other's purpose' (p. 133). The phrase '*made* to serve' does not mean 'physically forced to serve', and the phrase 'not for his own . . . purpose' does not mean that the man's actions are not self-interested. Hayek rightly points out that a man who acts under coercion still chooses so to act: a man who does what he is told at gunpoint still chooses to do it and he does it for his own good reasons, namely to stay alive. For Hayek a coercive situation is one where the coercer exploits the hopes and fears of the coerced in such a way that the latter, in acting self-interestedly within the situation which the former has created for him, also serves his coercer's purpose.

The trouble with this is that it seems to apply equally to many employer-employee situations. An employee is induced to serve his employer's purpose. True, Hayek regards 'the threat of inflicting harm' as an essential ingredient of a coercive situation; and the threats which an employer can use will be milder than those a gunman can use. Where unions are strong or full employment prevails an employer may hardly be in a position to threaten an employee at all. But there are still plenty of situations where an employee could be sacked and does not want to be sacked; and these would have to be classified as coercive situations on Hayek's definition.

My conclusion so far is that Hayek's definition of 'freedom' is both too wide and too narrow: too wide because it implies that the freedom of a man who feels bitterly frustrated by what he regards

* This terminology is due to R. Carnap. Speaking of the adequacy or inadequacy of some proposed definition or 'rational reconstruction' R of some concept or 'explicandum', he writes: 'Since the explicandum is vague (otherwise it would not require definition), there will be no general agreement for all cases . . .; but there are certain cases for which there is practical agreement that the explicandum holds, other cases for which there is practical agreement that it does not hold. . . . Now we might say that R is *clearly too wide* if we find cases in which R holds but the explicandum clearly (i.e. with practically general agreement) does not hold. And we might say that R is *clearly too narrow* if we find cases where R does not hold but the explicandum clearly holds. It is possible that R is clearly too wide in one direction and clearly too narrow in another' (*Logical Foundations of Probability*, 1950, p. 466).

as a stupid and immoral law is not infringed; and too narrow because it implies that a man who does a job from which he does not want to be sacked and which serves other people's purposes is unfree.

But Hayek adds some further ingredients to his definition of 'coercion'. He speaks of coercion as involving a person's mind being 'made someone else's tool', or involving the subjection of one man's will to another's (p. 135). I am not sure, however, how such remarks should be taken. From their context it seems that Hayek is not thinking of such things as brainwashing, hypnotic suggestions, and subliminal advertising, where a person's mind is, to some extent, under another's control. I think that what he means to indicate by such remarks is that, while the actions of a coerced person are voluntary, the result of his choice within the constraining situation in which he finds himself, they express his coercer's, rather than his own, intentions: 'the only comprehensive design that his actions fit into is that of another mind' (p. 134).

Again, it seems to me that this view of coercion is too wide. If we consider a worker who performs one simple operation in a complicated technological process which he does not understand, it will be true of him that the 'only comprehensive design that his actions fit into is that of another mind'.

Hayek also describes coercion as 'the control of the essential data of an individual's action by another' (p. 139), and he relates it to fraud and deception where, not the data themselves, but the agent's beliefs about them, are manipulated by another (p. 144). Again it seems to me that this is too wide. For example, it fits a worker on a building site who is for ever adjusting his activity to the foreman's directions. Hayek seems aware of this sort of objection, for he goes out of his way to insist that 'the employees of a plant will . . . be mostly occupied with the routine of carrying out standing orders, adapting them all the time to particular circumstances and only occasionally receiving specific commands' (pp. 150–1). He concedes that men become 'mere tools' in so far as they obey specific orders – fortunately, however, the rule of standing orders largely prevails in modern factories! But this suggests to me that the distinction between specific orders and standing orders cannot bear the great weight Hayek puts on it. If worker A has a completely routine job regulated entirely by standing orders, whereas worker B has to make frequent adjustments to a foreman's directions, this surely does not mean that A is free and B a slave?

Do these criticisms have any significance for Hayek's main argument? We saw that his definitions of 'freedom' and 'coercion' were motivated by his desire to assimilate civil laws and impersonal social forces to natural constraints, and to keep these sharply separated from personal commands, so that the conclusion could be drawn that in a competitive society enjoying a rule of law coercion would be minimised and freedom maximised. I think that the definitional difficulties we have been considering suggest that this assimilation is not altogether feasible. There is a large difference between a stupid civil law, however abstract and general and non-discriminatory, and a law of nature: the former has been made by men and can be unmade by men. On the other hand, there may be little difference, so far as freedom is concerned, between a standing order posted by the foreman on the works notice-board, and a series of specific instructions given by him to individual workers.

Moreover, while natural forces as such are non-coercive, a new element enters when someone is hit by a natural disaster which could have been humanly prevented. If contagious diseases spread because of the inefficiency of the public health service, people smitten by them may well feel that the government is largely responsible. The same is true of economic disasters. I agree that there is an important difference between being thrown out of work by the blind workings of the economic system, and being thrown into prison at the behest of an oriental despot. One cannot accuse a system of vindictiveness. But one may accuse a government of callousness or stupidity for allowing something avoidable to happen. In short, while I have nothing but admiration for Hayek's stern criticisms of those who have, in recent decades, been pouring cold (and muddy) water on the idea of a rule of law, and while I think that the distinction between personal control and the impersonal pressure exercised by civil and social forces is an important one, I nevertheless think that he is over-impressed by this distinction. For the fact is that for many impersonal phenomena certain persons are partly responsible; and if someone's life is dislocated by some such impersonal phenomenon, he may not be content to regard it as an act of God. He may very well regard those whose actions (or inaction) helped to cause (or allowed) it to happen with something of the bitterness with which he would have regarded someone who had caused a similar dislocation by personal coercion.

I think that what we really have is a scale with direct control of one person by another at one end and the laws of nature at the other, and with civil laws and 'impersonal' social processes coming somewhere in the middle. It is not only that the latter are man-made (if seldom or never the reflection of any one man's intention) and humanly alterable which inclines me to place them in the middle. There is also the consideration that they, unlike natural laws, operate through personal decisions. Some official has to *decide* to prosecute before the criminal law can come into operation. If bad economic conditions oblige an employer to lay off workers, he must decide just how many and *which.* A landlord whose tenants have got into arrears with the rent must decide whether or not to allow them any more grace. True, all these decisions would be circumscribed by prevailing conditions, but not so narrowly as to leave no room for personal discretion. Social processes have only a quasi-impersonal character, and do not proceed in the completely automatic manner of natural processes.

Responsibility

Hayek would probably not wish to deny that his attitude to many questions is tinged by pragmatism, and even by positivism. There are indications in *The Constitution of Liberty* that he is inclined to appraise moral values in terms of their conduciveness 'to the continued existence of our society' (p. 36; and see p. 67); and he happily accepts the positivist claim that the problem of free-will *v.* determinism is a pseudo-problem, and also the associated pragmatic theory of responsibility.

None of this is congenial to me. I shall say nothing here about the problem of the free-will problem.* I will concentrate on his view of moral responsibility.

Since responsibility is interpreted by Hayek within a determinist setting, to say that a man is responsible for his action cannot mean, for Hayek, that he was the causal initiator of his act or that he could have acted otherwise. Then what does it mean? Hayek answers:

* Except to say that I think it was a little misleading of Hayek to tuck in a reference without comment to C. A. Campbell's famous article, 'Is Free Will a Pseudo-Problem?' (*Mind*, 1951), which is a powerful and incisive criticism of the pseudo-problem thesis, among a list of writings supporting that thesis.

> 'Rather, the statement that a person is responsible for what he does aims at making his actions different from what they would be if he did not believe it to be true. We assign responsibility to a man, not in order to say that as he was he might have acted differently, but in order to make him different . . .
>
> The only questions that can be legitimately raised, therefore, are whether the person upon whom we place responsibility for a particular action . . . is . . . accessible to normal motives . . . [and] can be expected to be influenced. . . in a desirable direction' (p. 75).*

On this view, a man will be more responsible the more amenable he is to external persuasion. An utterly stubborn man, impervious to all external influences, would not be responsible at all (but akin to the obsessional neurotic).

Now let us turn to Hayek's view of coercability and inner strength:

> 'Whether or not attempts to coerce a particular person will be successful depends in a large measure on that person's inner strength . . . we may pity the weak or very sensitive person whom a mere frown may "compel" to do what he would not do otherwise' (p. 138).

I do not claim that there is a formal contradiction between his view of responsibility and his view of coercability; but I do think there is a conflict of appraisals here. He wants people to be as responsible as possible and believes that a free society fosters responsibility more than any other (p. 76). He also admires people of inner strength who resist attempts to coerce them. Yet he comes close to defining a person's degree of responsibility in terms of his degree of coercability.

I find the pragmatic theory of responsibility inherently implausible. Not only does it have counter-intuitive results when applied to stubborn saints and sinners, and trainable domestic pets,† but it shares with a purely deterrent theory of punishment the peculiarity of turning statements which are essentially related to historical events into purely forward-looking utterances. It would generally be agreed that if a man is held responsible for causing or allowing something bad to happen, this charge refers backwards in time to that bad happening and his relation to it. It would also generally be agreed that such a charge might be *refuted*, perhaps by showing that what happened was the least bad alternative in the circumstances,

* I have made considerable omissions from this passage.
† See M. Cranston, *Freedom: a new analysis*, p. 155.

or that the man could not have reasonably foreseen that it would result from his well-meaning actions. But according to the pragmatic theory of responsibility, such a charge is not a refutable statement about the past at all; indeed it is not even a *statement* and so is not refutable. It is only an utterance intended to have a causal influence on future events, an inoculation against negligence and bad behaviour.

A final objection to this theory is that it relies on not being generally accepted. A psychiatrist's confidence-bolstering talk is likely to misfire if his patient suspects that the psychiatrist does not mean it and is only trying to bolster his confidence with it. Similarly, responsibility-talk is likely to misfire if the recipient believes (as he ought to, according to the pragmatic theory of responsibility) that he is merely being got at. If the pragmatic theory of responsibility were generally accepted, responsibility-talk would no longer be useful.

But I must not conclude this section without a word of praise for the admirable passage where Hayek demands that a person's responsibility should be commensurate with his capacities and castigates a modern tendency to make each of us 'responsible' for all the ills of the world.

> 'To be effective, responsibility must be both definite and limited. . . It is quite as destructive of any sense of responsibility to be taught that one is responsible for everything as to be taught that one cannot be held responsible for anything' (p. 83).

The justification of freedom

Hayek is very severe on the English utilitarians. They were false individualists who paved the way for socialism. Yet there seems to be a good deal in common between his position and theirs. They too insisted that the state's functions are severely limited by human ignorance. For instance, the state may not pretend to know better than an individual what would make him happiest. Again, although they did not stress this as much as Hayek does, they agreed that we seldom know enough to decide single cases on their singular merits, that we should rather decide them according to general rules, these alone being judged by results. Like Hayek, they had a considerable (though not uncritical) confidence in a market economy, and a strong hostility to monopolies (Bentham would have read Hayek's chapter on trade unions with the keenest pleasure). And like Hayek, they appraised things in a pretty pragmatic way.

J. S. Mill wrote in the introductory chapter of his *Liberty:*

> 'It is proper to state that I forego any advantage which could be derived to my argument from the idea of abstract right . . . I regard utility as the ultimate appeal on all ethical questions; but it must be utility in the largest sense, grounded on the permanent interests of a man as a progressive being.'

Hayek writes in the introductory chapter of his *The Constitution of Liberty:*

> 'Some readers will perhaps be disturbed by the impression that I do not take the value of individual liberty as an indisputable ethical presupposition and that, in trying to demonstrate its value, I am possibly making the argument in its support a matter of expediency. This would be a misunderstanding. But it is true that if we want to convince those who do not already share our moral suppositions, we must not simply take them for granted' (p. 6).

In the case of both Mill and Hayek we can only applaud their decision to *argue* the case for liberty, with the result that we have two books full of sober and important reasoning, whereas they could hardly have spun out to book-length the assertion that we just have a natural right to liberty, or that the value of liberty is just an indisputable ethical presupposition.

Yet a certain risk is involved in such argumentation. If I believe that honesty is the morally right policy, and someone denies this, then it will indeed be futile for me just to go on insisting that the rightness of honesty is a God-given datum. I should produce some arguments. But I must be careful. Suppose I argue that honesty is the best policy, i.e. that in the long run it is more profitable to be honest. That might shake him; and once I had shaken him, I might go on to produce arguments of a different character. But if I argued *only* that honesty is the best policy, I might defeat my purpose, for I might give the impression that it is not honesty but profitability that I regard as of supreme importance so that *if* honesty turned out, after all, *not* to be the best policy, I would drop honesty.

Hayek conducts his argument in terms of the 'benefits' of freedom;* and the benefits he points to are enormous. There has been a good

* See pp. 31–2; p. 53 (where he argues that, in view of the awakening of backward nations, failure to maintain the rate of material progress made possible by economic freedom 'might be fatal to us'); and p. 394 ('the ultimate aim of freedom is the enlargement of those capacities in which man surpasses his ancestors and to which each generation must endeavour to add its share').

deal of bogus talk recently about the *angst* and loneliness of people in a free society and the comforts of paternalism – as though friendship and laughter and sexual happiness come more easily under the eye of authority. It is good to be shown that the boot is on the other foot. It is as if, word having got round that honesty, though morally required of us, is a painful policy, someone were to show the enormous advantages of honesty.

Yet I wish that Hayek had taken care to explain that he was showing that there is only a happy coincidence between the moral value and the social benefits of freedom, and that he was not arguing that freedom is valuable simply *because* of its social benefits.

This brings me to my last point. To bring out the moral significance of freedom one has, I think, to employ a wider concept of freedom than Hayek does. Not being terrorised, bullied, pushed around by petty officials; being regulated only by known laws; making one's own mistakes – all this is, of course, quite essential. But it is not the whole story. Hayek brushes aside talk about 'inner' freedom (p. 15); and certainly the Platonic-Rousseauist illustration he gives is unacceptable. Still, it *is* possible for someone to be terrorised, bullied and pushed around by imaginary fears and anxieties and ignorant prejudices; and his condition *may* be about as miserable, in a different way, as that of, say, a political prisoner of a totalitarian régime who has no outer freedom at all but who sustains himself by refusing to compromise and by using all his intelligence to find out how the system he is caught in works and how he might outwit it.

Hayek says that his aim was to make 'a comprehensive restatement of the basic principles of a philosophy of freedom' (p. 3); and he has certainly provided very strong social, economic and juristic arguments against coercion. But I feel that something is missing which stops it being a *comprehensive* restatement. The condition of a man's soul also matters.

ARTHUR A. SHENFIELD

Economic Director of the Federation of British Industries since 1955. Assistant Editor of the London & Cambridge Economic Service, 1937–40. Lecturer in Economics at the University of Birmingham, 1940–8. Barrister-at-Law of Gray's Inn and in active practice at the English Bar, 1946–55. In 1949–50 he was Economic Adviser to the Government of Trinidad, and since then he has been consulted by other governments in the British Caribbean and has sat as Chairman of Commissions of Enquiry into economic problems in that region. From 1955–60 he was Chairman of the Finance Committee of the Imperial College of Tropical Agriculture, Trinidad. He has lectured widely on British economic affairs in the U.S.A., Canada, Mexico, New Zealand and the Continent.

III

Law

A. A. SHENFIELD

The Constitution of Liberty is one of the great books of our time, profound in analysis, ample in scholarship, noble in spirit. It is masterly in all its parts. So complete a study of its subject could be attempted by few men in our world, and fewer still would be likely to match the success which Professor Hayek achieves. All this ought to be said by way of preamble, whichever section of the book is submitted to examination.

Certainly the section on law, taken in the round, is an achievement of an extremely high order. It may be that the most fundamental, and perhaps also the most profound, passages in the book are those concerned with the meaning and value of freedom. Those, however, which are the most important for the understanding of how men must act together to preserve and extend freedom in society are naturally concerned with law; and when one stands back and surveys the edifice which Hayek has erected in this section one is inspired by the rightness of his design.

If this preamble is followed by a warning that there are faults in the book and that some criticism is justifiable, it is not to be construed as a reviewer's attempt to impress his readers with the keenness of his judicial eye. It is in fact difficult to find anything so far awry in Hayek's treatment of law as seriously to endanger his main argument. The faults arise partly from compression; partly from a tendency to suggest that one can get nearer to a completely satisfying solution for certain problems of law and its nature than in fact is possible; and partly because the rule of law, which as one would expect is at the heart of Hayek's exposition, is an ideal, not capable in practice of universal or of uniformly precise application. Where ideals are concerned, there is room for reasonable disagreement on how near it is possible to approach them, and hence on whether the fault for a failure to reach them may not lie in the ideals themselves as well as in men; but Hayek gives this not inconsiderable difficulty only passing consideration.

The Hayekian analysis

Here are the essentials of Hayek's exposition.

First, laws are general, abstract rules. They are distinguished from commands party because of these qualities of generality and abstraction and partly also, and this is more important, because they differ in effect and purpose. In purpose and effect a command imposes the will of one man over another. The source of the action which results from it is the will of the commander. Laws are different. Of course they limit, and sometimes prescribe, action. But when they limit action, the source of whatever is done is the will of the actor, rather than that of the lawgiver; and even when they prescribe action they do so in general in respect of hypothetical situations which may or may not arise or which the citizen may bypass if they do arise. Thus even laws which prescribe action leave the citizen an area of freedom within which he may choose whether to act or not. It is true that in practice commands merge into law and laws into commands, but this does not prevent us from recognising the attributes of true law, namely generality and abstraction. As a result of these attributes true laws produce and preserve freedom, for they set up a fence around a stronghold in which each man may decide for himself what to do with his life, what wants to satisfy, what purposes to serve and how to do so. This is what is meant by 'the government of laws, not of men' which, despite the sophisticated ridicule of 'liberals',* has continued to live vigorously in the American tradition. If what passes for law is in fact command, the citizen's stronghold cannot be made impregnable and his freedom is undermined.

Secondly, the laws of a free society must conform to the rule of law, at least as far as coercion is concerned. The rule of law is a general rule, but it is not that kind of general rule which is a defini-

* In the American sense. The capture by American social-democrats of the splendid name 'liberal' is a disaster. The effective loss of the word 'democratic' to the so-called 'people's democracies' of Eastern Europe would not be worse.

tion of law itself. Thus it is not in fact a law but a rule about what the law ought to be, or perhaps less ambiguously, about what characteristics the law ought to have. Hence, as Hayek styles it, it is a meta-legal doctrine or a political ideal. While generality and abstraction are sufficient to establish a 'law' as true law, laws which conform to the rule of law display two other major characteristics, namely predictability and impartiality (a safer word than equality, which must constantly be followed in this context, implicitly or explicitly, by the words 'before the law' lest it be confused with the substantive equality which is its enemy). Because such laws are predictable, the citizen knows what his legal environment is and so he can plan his life without fear of the caprice of his rulers in pronouncing what the law is. Because the laws are impartial (which must include their application as well as their content) he can proceed without fear of caprice in the measurement of his deserts against those of others.*

As the rule of law is a political ideal and not a law, it is not to be expected that laws can always pass its tests unscathed. Thus 'many of its applications are also ideals which we can hope to approach very closely but can never fully realise' (pp. 205–6). As Hayek has said on a previous occasion:

> 'It is thus quite possible that in fact none of these principles can be applied in all its ultimate consequences. What we are dealing with is ideals which we can approach in greater or less degree; but how near we get to these ideals depends upon how far they are generally regarded as worthy. If they are presented as illusions and men cease to strive to realise them, their practical influence must quickly fade away.'†

Thus the effectiveness of the rule of law depends upon the measure of belief in it. This in turn depends upon the measure of belief in individual liberty and the degree of acceptance of the analysis which aims to show that individual liberty can be preserved only by laws which conform to the rule of law.

* All this was stated simply in *The Road to Serfdom* (page 54), viz. 'Stripped of all technicalities this means that government in all its actions is bound by rules fixed and announced beforehand – rules which make it possible to foresee with fair certainty how the authority will use its coercive powers in given circumstances and to plan one's individual affairs on the basis of this knowledge'.

† *Wirtschaft ohne Wunder*, Eugen Rentsch, 1953.

Thirdly, *pace* Dicey, the rule of law does not exclude the possibility of setting up a special administrative law. Indeed it may require it. Nor does it exclude the exercise of administrative power or the delegation of administrative responsibility. What matters is not that power is delegated or is in the hands of administrators rather than legislators, but that it should be exercised according to rules which are general, predictable and impartial.

Fourthly, the history of the rule of law shows the prime importance of constitutionalism and federalism. Despite the example of Britain, which is a very special case, it is very difficult to preserve liberty unless those who have power to legislate at any given moment are subject to general rules which express the more permanent purposes of the state. The constitution stands in relation to the legislative power in a way somewhat similar to that in which a particular law stands in relation to the judge who must construe it. The freedom to legislate within the constitution is analogous to the freedom of construction of the law available to the judge. As liberty powerfully limits the scope of state action it is most likely to be menaced by the urges of the moment, when some great aim incompatible with liberty seizes the mind of men. Hence a constitution which upholds the long-considered and, if it has persisted for any length of time, the well-tried, aims of the people forces the legislators to restrain these urges.

Federalism is as much a part of the monumental American contribution to the theory and practice of liberty as is constitutionalism. The essence of federalism is that it breaks up power. The separation of power between the executive and legislative branches of government (and of course obviously the separation of these two from the judicial branch) is valuable, despite the revisions which have had to be made in its classic statement and despite the fact that everywhere some agency (e.g. the party system) arises to recombine the two. But the separation of responsibilities among different territorial authorities which results from federalism is in some ways a better method of preventing the concentration of power, and perhaps one more likely to persist. In a federation no single government is competent to act over the whole field of executive responsibility, and so there are always likely to be havens for minorities to have concurrent power with majorities, and not merely to have the hope of some day becoming majorities, valuable though that is. Though federalism obviously is not a *sine qua non* of liberty, it is an example of prime importance of the methods by which liberty may be preserved.

The history of the rule of law also brings to light the important contribution to the problems of liberty of German lawyers in the eighteenth and nineteenth centuries. So far from being backward in their understanding of the legal postulates and requirements of liberty, German legal theorists until fairly recently perhaps went furthest of all in designs for the application of the rule of law when they fashioned programmes for a *Rechtsstaat*.* It is one of the great tragedies of modern history that, being engulfed by the tide of anti-liberalism well before Western Europe, Germany succumbed to notions hostile to the rule of law just as her scholars' ideas on the *Rechtsstaat* displayed their full flowering.

Fifthly, the rule of law excludes state action of the kind variously called 'economic planning', '*dirigisme*', or 'interventionism'. It also excludes policies intended to redistribute wealth, as distinct from alleviating poverty. This is because state action of this kind must conflict with the canons of generality, predictability, and impartiality – generality and impartiality because such action cannot be taken without discrimination between individuals or groups of individuals, and predictability because the centralisation of economic initiative required cannot be effective without the daily or hourly exercise of decision over prices, production and consumption which no one, not even the servants of the state themselves, can foresee. But of course the rule of law is not incompatible with the control of the economy through a legal framework within which economic initiative amongst the citizens is decentralised. State action of this kind is a requirement, not a breach, of the rule.

With the exception of the acclaim given to the theorists of the *Rechtsstaat*, this is all familiar to readers of English and American writings in this field. Of course it is not surprising, for Hayek's case is that the fundamentals of freedom under law were expounded long ago, above all by the Whig philosophers and the classical economists.†

* I.e. a state conforming to the rule of law. In its last stages the concept embodied the functioning of a system of administrative law and administrative courts in order to control the apparatus of administration.

† Above all, and best of all, by Hume; but of course also by Locke, Adam Smith, Burke, Paley and many others.

The nature of law

Let us examine the argument as he presents it. First, the nature of law. It is a commonplace that there are deep, possibly insoluble, problems here. No doubt laws in developed societies are nearly always general rules and hence they satisfy the test of abstraction. But is this not because the complexity of developed societies makes government by command extremely difficult? Where a command is clothed with legality, it seems to me difficult to maintain that it cannot properly be called a law on the ground that it is not of a general character. It is possible to take the view that in his extremely eloquent chapter on the nature of law Hayek runs a little ahead of himself and applies the ideal of the rule of law to the discussion of the nature of law. He is of course right in deriding the view that the rule of law is satisfied if any law or command bears the mark of legality.* This is the contention of those who do not believe in the rule. But though legality alone cannot make a law satisfy the rule of law, it may be enough as a qualification for law itself. It is not foolish to say that law is what is accepted as law (which is not the same as saying that it is approved, or even obeyed, by those who accept it). Now it may be that what is accepted as law in any given case is not only general and abstract in character but is accepted as law for that reason. This still does not establish the proposition that only a general and abstract rule can be law.

It may be said that legality is an uncertain, as well as superficial, quality. Mere legal forms are not enough. The authority of the law-givers must also be accepted, and this may raise many difficulties for the theorist of law. Qualities of generality and abstraction may be said to be more fundamental. Perhaps they are, but they cannot be said to be more certain than legality. And in any case they cannot be accepted as criteria of what law is simply because they are valid criteria of what a particular law ought to be.

If it is justified, this may appear to be a damaging criticism of Hayek's exposition. I do not think it is. Discussions of the nature of law are notoriously sterile. What matters is not what law is but what laws ought to be. Hence to import the rule of law as a test of the

* E.g. 'The Hitlerite State, equally with that of Great Britain or France, is a Rechtstaat in the sense that dictatorial power has been transferred to the Führer by legal order.' Laski in 'The State in Theory and Practice', pp. 177–178. The same view is presented in other writings such as those of Sir Ivor Jennings, W. A. Robson, Herman Finer, W. L. Friedmann and numerous others.

nature of law may be wrong, but it does not affect Hayek's vital conclusions.

However, there seems to me to be one point, of possibly moderate importance, in this section of his argument which Hayek perhaps disposes of too lightly. He recognises that even general, abstract, rules, equally applicable to all, may be oppressive, but he thinks that this is unimportant in practice. He may be right. Perhaps oppressive, though impartial, sumptuary legislation or theocratic rule is improbable except in simple societies quite unlike modern complex societies; yet Prohibition was enacted in twentieth-century America, and in the realm of the mind there is much that is tyrannical in the Communist countries that the rulers apply to themselves as well as to the ruled. What matters is that even complete generality and impartiality are not absolute bars to oppression. But this brings us to the rule of law.

As I have said, the rule is an ideal. Because the rule is 'only' an ideal, many of its opponents take comfort. They can rightly say that champions of ideals notoriously dismiss evidence of their inapplicability to the real world as simply a failure of men to live up to them. Further there is a variety of competing ideals to choose from. Thus Sir Ivor Jennings could say 'The rule of law in this sense* is a rule of action for Whigs and may be ignored by others'.† However, dismissing Dicey as a Whig would be a way of relegating him to a dead past were it not that it is a question of Whig ideals, not party interests, against other ideals; and whether Whig ideals are dead or not is a different question from whether they ought to be. Sir Ivor no doubt intended to dismiss the rule as out of date, but in fact, perhaps unwittingly, he put it on the plane of competing ideals. On this plane Hayek's discussion is superb; it would perhaps be enough to bring his readers with him into the Whig camp were it not that something else needs attention.

What matters when we recognize the rule of law to be 'only' an ideal is whether the result of attempting to follow it, among men who are not saints or supermen, can differ from that of not doing so by a margin which is large and recognisable even where it cannot be followed completely; or whether the exceptions and shortfalls must be so frequent or important that the ideal ceases to be a

* I.e. the sense in which Dicey thought it ought to be a principle of policy.
† *The Law and the Constitution*, 5th edition, p. 308.

practical guide. I wish that Hayek had addressed himself to this question, for none could have dealt with it more faithfully. There is not much doubt that the answer would be favourable to the rule of law.

Predictability and impartiality of law

Let us consider the requirements of predictability and impartiality. These have been the main objects of attack by the opponents of the rule of law, and predictability in particular.* The arguments are of a wide range of quality. Two types can be dismissed at once. They would be hardly worth noticing were it not that they are explicit or implicit in most of the writings of lawyers with a bias to the Left, such as Sir Ivor Jennings, Professor W. A. Robson and the late Professor Harold J. Laski.†

One is the familiar gambit that predictability and impartiality cannot now produce justice because they thwart modern ideas of justice. The world has changed and laws and judges have changed, or ought to change, with it. It is an argument advanced when one likes the change and opposed when one does not. The complexity of the modern economy, the climate of opinion in favour of state interventionism, the mobilisation or semi-mobilisation of our times, have demanded and produced a transformation of society. If society has been transformed, ideas of justice must be transformed with it. The argument is of course contemptible, but how revealing it is of the intellectual content of collectivism, which has an almost automatic tendency to regard the trend of the times as its own justification even when it is that trend itself which is under scrutiny!

* See especially, for example, W. L. Friedmann in *Law and Social Change in Contemporary Britain* and *Law in a Changing Society* (both published by Stevens). It is interesting to see that the important branch of English law, namely equity, which began as a power of discretion to dispense natural justice, has become as completely formalised and subject to rule and precedent as law (in the narrow sense distinguishable from equity) itself. It is true that the voice of Denning, L. J. (now Lord Denning) has been heard to call for a new equity which will restore something of the Lord Chancellor's original discretion (Presidential Address to the Bentham Club, 1952), but it has found hardly an echo amongst other lawyers. Measuring justice according to the length of someone's foot, whether it be the Lord Chancellor's or not, is fortunately not acceptable in a society which still has respect for freedom under law.

† In some respects, e.g. the use of administrative tribunals to further social policies unhampered by the rule of law, the views of such writers have been approved by Conservative lawyers in a symposium, *Liberty in the Modern State*, Conservative Political Centre, 1957. See Maitland's definition of the Star Chamber below, p. 60.

The second is that the predictability of law, even if it could be ensured, is of little value if the citizen is left, in the things that most matter to him, to be blown hither and thither by the unpredictable winds of the free market. The 'planning' state, it is said, gives effective predictability in his daily life, while if it is democratic its administrative machinery is checked by rules and procedures which prevent oppression. This is partly a variant of the 'freedom is no use to a starving man' type of argument, and partly the result of a most unjudicial examination of the powers of administrators and administrative tribunals.

The respectable arguments about predictability and impartiality centre around the problem of judicial discretion. Consider the following two dicta.

> 'The words he (i.e. the judge) must construe are empty vessels into which he can put nearly anything he will': Judge Learned Hand.
>
> 'The prophecies of what the courts will do in fact and nothing more pretentious, are what I mean by the law': Mr. Justice Oliver Wendell Holmes.

Taken literally Learned Hand's view of the function of the judge is almost that of a cadi dispensing palm tree justice.* There can be little predictability here; and if the rule of law rests on predictability it rests on quicksands. Holmes's view is of course not the same. To have to prophesy what the courts will do on the basis of given facts does not mean that the courts are not bound by pre-existing codes or by authoritative precedents. But it throws doubt on the possibility of any high degree of predictability in practice.

There are two separate problems here. One arises from the fact that laws cannot be wholly certain. They are drafted, made and construed by fallible men. Judges are not only fallible in construing laws which are ambiguous or obscure; they are also to some extent the children of their times. Thus judgments on certain types of cases change with the times. And of course the assessment of facts in any given case, whether by judge or by jury, is always a matter into which chance enters.

* Of course this does not truly represent Judge Hand's view of the function of a judge, still less his own fine practice. He had in mind here the uncertain provisions of constitutional law. He was also lapsing somewhat unjudicially into exaggeration.

Professor Hayek is right here in drawing attention to a measure of conflict of principle between case law systems and the rule of law. Codes are, at least at first sight, much more consistent with the rule.* But he is also right, though I think with not quite enough analysis, in rejecting the uncertainty of law and the fallibility of the judicial process as grounds for rejecting the principle of predictability. In the western world we all know that our laws are broadly predictable to quite a high degree, though most of us also know that there are hazards in getting into court (most of the hazards, however, arising from disputed questions of fact). And nations with long memories know that there have been other systems of much less predictability, not to mention those now existing in totalitarian countries. Most Englishmen would still approve of Maitland's description of the Court of Star Chamber and treat it as a condemnation: viz., 'a court of politicians enforcing a policy, not a court of judges administering the law'.

The second problem arises from judicial discretion of another kind (indeed the only true discretion, for judicial fallibility in the construction of the law is not strictly the result of a discretionary power). Within limits judges have a free hand in passing sentence on convicted offenders, and in certain cases juries or judges have a free hand in awarding civil damages. In divorce suits in England judges have a discretion to refuse a decree if the petitioner's own marital offences are not fully disclosed. As a good deal is made of this field of discretion by some writers,† it merits consideration. Damage awards may be dismissed at once. There is a true discretion only in cases of exemplary damages and these are rare (and even there the discretion is limited). The uncertainty about damages in other cases is simply a facet of the difficulty of predicting the assessment of facts. Dis-

* It is doubtful whether this is so in practice. Codes as well as decided cases call for construction, and where there are lacunae a judge not bound by precedent may exercise a more unpredictable discretion. 'Judge-made' law may arise in either case. However, it must be admitted that in the English system judges still have a vestigial power to make law in a more open sense, e.g. in R. *v.* Manley (1933 1KB 529), where the court in effect created the offence of 'public mischief'. Consider also the claim made for a power in the Courts to construe the common law in such a way as to safeguard public morals where this is not done by statute, per Lord Simonds in Shaw v. Director of Public Prosecutions, *The Times*, 5th May, 1961. It is impossible to reconcile this with the rule of the law. Still, it may have its counterpart in codified systems, e.g. the Swiss Code of 1907 which enjoined the judges to act when faced with uncertainty as if they were legislators.

† Notably Friedmann. See *Law and Social Change*, pp. 294–6 and *Law in a Changing Society*, pp. 24–62.

cretion in divorce suits may also be dismissed. However wide it may have been in the past, it is now so confined by rule (admittedly judge-made) that there can hardly be any element of unpredictability or partiality in it. It is only in the case of sentences that there is a truly wide judicial discretion.

Now it is true that this introduces a large measure of unpredictability for the citizen who is contemplating what the law permits and forbids; though of course punishments are partly limited by statute and he knows that normally a rough and ready scale is applied within the statutory limits. Yet it is extremely doubtful whether the unpredictability of sentences is relevant to the arguments for and against the rule of law. The walls around the citizen's stronghold of freedom are maintained on the footing that he obeys the law. If he transgresses it, he must properly rely on mercy as well as justice; and mercy must be more unpredictable than justice. Or to put it another way, his deserts as an offender are in reality a question of fact and the discretion of the judge is not really a discretion but a duty, which by the nature of things produces unpredictable results, to assess this fact.

Thus though numberless volumes have been written on the nature of the judicial process by the enemies of the rule of law, their efforts amount to no more than the exaggeration, sometimes grotesque, of these shortfalls in predictability and impartiality.* In practice we know that laws and their enforcement can achieve a high enough mark from the tests of the rule of law to be significantly different from those that fail. Hence the rule survives as a practical ideal.

Administrative powers and administrative law

With perhaps one qualification, and subject to the needs of compression, Hayek's treatment of the problem of administrative powers and administrative law seems to me to be wholly admirable. The discussion in England of these matters has been voluminous in the extreme but often beside the essential point which Hayek expounds so well. *The New Despotism* of Lord Chief Justice Hewart was timely but excitable. The Donoughmore Committee's treatment of

* Despite much compression Hayek deals admirably with legal positivists and historicists. He gives only passing mention to the 'free law' school and the school of 'jurisprudence of interest'.

the problems raised by Hewart was inadequate and myopic.* And in earlier days Dicey's classic statement of the rule of law was marred by his notorious misunderstanding of continental systems of administrative law. The one doubt I have about Professor Hayek's exposition relates to the impact of administrative powers on policy concerning the centralisation or decentralisation of economic initiative. It is true that the principles of generality, predictability and impartiality can be applied to the delegation of administrative powers; and it is also true that most of such powers which can conform to these principles will leave individual economic freedom unharmed. But not all. I wish Hayek had devoted some space to a discussion on those administrative powers which can in themselves conform to these principles and yet will undermine the rule of law because they hobble the working of the free market.

On the question of special administrative laws and courts, Hayek's view will be acceptable to modern authorities, who in recent years have brought to English minds a better understanding of the nature and working of continental systems of the *droit administratif.* This is not to say that Dicey deserves all the castigation which it is now customary to administer to him. It is interesting to see that the pioneers of the *Rechtsstaat* looked to the ordinary courts of the land to deal with administrative cases, and that it was only at a late stage that special administrative courts were envisaged as a feature of the *Rechtsstaat*. Still it must be admitted that Dicey gravely misunderstood the *droit administratif* of his day and was excessively impressed by inessential defects in its practice. As Hayek says:

> 'By his attempt to vindicate the rule of law as he saw it,† Dicey in effect blocked the development which would have offered the best chance of preserving it. He could not stop the growth in the Anglo-Saxon world of an administrative apparatus similar to that which existed on the Continent. But he did contribute much to prevent or delay the growth of institutions which could subject the new bureaucratic machinery to effective control' (p. 204).

* Even though it paid lip-service to the rule of law the Committee bears a heavy responsibility for the blindness to the dangers of unchecked administrative discretion which developed in Britain in the 1930's. The hand of Harold Laski – a prominent and vocal member – can be seen in much of the Committee's Report.

† But it is only in the part concerned with the role of the ordinary courts and law of the land that Dicey's statement of the rule of law is seriously defective.

Constitutionalism and federalism

What Hayek says about constitutionalism and federalism is of the highest importance for English readers. Our experience is a very special one, and it is easy for us to adopt an air of superiority when we contemplate those who place their trust in written constitutions and federal arrangements. In both cases Hayek seems to me to be right in stressing their significance for freedom, and here too his exposition is in all fundamentals of the highest quality. In the case of constitutionalism there are only two points where I detect some weakness. First it seems to me to have been unwise to use the analogy of the law and the judge's powers of construing it in explaining the relation between the constitution and the powers of legislators. The cases are not on all fours, except in a sense which is too deceptively simple, and the analogy is unnecessary for the understanding of the constitutional limits on legislative powers. Secondly Hayek ventilates but does not solve the problem of whether the American Supreme Court should have the power to declare unconstitutional laws which they judge to be contrary to the spirit of the constitution though not in terms forbidden by it. He obviously leans to the view that they should, but he does not venture on a full discussion of what is, of course, a profoundly difficult and perplexing matter. There is of course a sense in which the spirit of the constitution should breathe in every Supreme Court judgment, but I think that the preponderant view of those who would in general count themselves Hayek's admirers and supporters would be that the court followed the path of wisdom when it accepted the doctrine that it could declare unconstitutional only those laws which were clearly outside the written limits of the constitution. Nevertheless Hayek is right to draw attention to the difficulties which this produced for the court as the guardian of the constitution.

Federalism as a principle raises no great excitement among English readers, but as its greatest current test concerns the rights of negroes in the Southern States it tends to be rather unpopular with them. This makes it all the more desirable that the arguments in its favour should receive proper attention. Hayek is here in the excellent company of Lord Acton, who was a convinced supporter of the Southern States' claims for States' Rights before the Civil War. That the Southern States seek to deny the full rights of citizenship to a section of their people only means that in a federation some of the governments may follow foolish or unjust policies, which is irrelevant to the case for federalism. If folly and injustice are at large it is well that there should be more than one government for them to conquer before they prevail. In fact, if the Southern States' policies are unconstitutional, they will not succeed and the power of the Federal Government will prevail, however slowly. What matters is that in an age of pressure for the extension of governmental powers in social and economic affairs, the Americans have a built-in system for splitting these powers even while they are extended; or, if the pressure is for centralising them, a built-in system of resistance to it.

State economic action

At last we come to what for our times is the most important question of all. What kind of state action in the economic field is compatible with freedom under law and what is not? Professor Hayek's position is well known. It was expounded with beautiful clarity in *The Road to Serfdom*, and the discussion in *The Constitution of Liberty* follows the same lines, but with elaboration of the relevance of the rule of law. Hayek's views on economic policy are dealt with at length elsewhere in this volume and my concern is only with the argument concerning the application to state economic action of the tests of the rule of law. Subject to its proper limitations Hayek's case is, and always has been, irrefutable. What is debatable is the scope of the limitations; but as this is a common feature of political and economic theories, it seems to me that much of the disputation about *The Road to Serfdom* amongst liberals (in the European sense) would have been avoided or muted if it had been recognised.

Government control of the economy which involves the centralisation of economic initiative must conflict with the rule of law. Those who must decide over a large part of the economic field what is to be bought, what is to be sold, what is to be invested, and on what terms, must deal with unpredictable situations; and they must deal with them not according to pre-existing laws but according to the needs and judgments of the moment. Otherwise chaos or stagnation will ensue. Hence *dirigisme* on any scale must prevent state action from conforming with the rule of law. As for the redistribution of incomes, it may not be intended to produce the centralisation of economic initiative, but if it is on a substantial scale it will in fact go far to do so. For it undermines the incentives and thwarts the motives which make the free economy work, and then the centralising state is called in to give purpose and direction to it – destroying its freedom in the process.

It must be understood that the process may begin in a manner broadly compatible with the rule of law. The redistribution of incomes as such can be made quite consistent with the rule; it is its ultimate consequences which count. An interesting example is that of rent restriction laws. They are not a case of uncontrolled administrative powers for they operate according to due process of law, and the extent of judicial discretion provided by them is not great. Baffling though their construction is, the British courts have applied them with the utmost respect for the principles selected for Hayek's praise. Yet the miserable folly of these laws does grave harm to the free economy, and would undermine it and the rule of law with it if extended to other important fields.

However, if we are told that a certain course is incompatible with the rule of law, and the rule of law is itself an ideal which its most faithful supporters cannot fully realise, a good deal clearly depends upon relative magnitudes. To grope one's way on the road to serfdom is not the same as to race headlong along it; and this is not just because one goes less far to destruction but because one has a much better chance of changing one's mind and reversing one's direction, or perhaps of reaching a balance between the will to go and the will to return somewhere well short of the end of the road. Thus it is that so formidable a champion of the free enterprise system as Henry Wallich* is able to protest that Hayek's fears have proved groundless. The American economy has been subjected to a good deal of interventionism, but America remains free and the rule of law broadly prevails. But when Hayek wrote *The Road to Serfdom* Britain, which he had mainly in mind, was doing much more than groping her way to serfdom. And if the question at issue is the direction of movement, it is desirable that we should know where we are going. If others are racing along the road, still more if ignorance of our direction can cause us to go headlong, it is vital that we should know it. Thus Hayek's warnings have done us an inestimable service even though, in the full knowledge of what we are doing, we may be safe in ignoring them up to a point.

* *The Cost of Freedom*, Harper & Bros., 1960.

The problem of monopoly

There is one problem of state economic action which even some of Hayek's supporters would say raises a difficulty for his analytical position. It is the familiar problem of monopoly. It is not sufficient to say that the proper function of the state is to set up the framework of law within which men can go freely about their business. What is to be done if no framework of law can alone dissolve monopoly positions? Then some kind of direct intervention may be said to be necessary to preserve the freedom of enterprise which in general requires the state to refrain from direct intervention.

Although Hayek excuses himself from a full discussion of this problem, his compressed treatment of it appears to me to be splendidly pithy and to the point. I cannot do better than quote him, almost in full.

> '. . . it may be a good thing if the monopolist is treated as a sort of whipping boy of economic policy; and I recognise that, in the United States, legislation has succeeded in creating a climate of opinion unfavourable to monopoly. . . . I have become increasingly sceptical, however, about the beneficial character of any discretionary action of government against particular monopolies, and I am seriously alarmed at the arbitrary nature of all policy aimed at limiting the size of individual enterprises. And when policy creates a state of affairs in which, as is true of some enterprises in the United States, large firms are afraid to compete by lowering prices because this may expose them to antitrust action, it becomes an absurdity.
>
> Current policy fails to recognise that it is not monopoly as such, or bigness, but only obstacles to entry into an industry or trade and certain other monopolistic practices that are harmful. Monopoly is certainly undesirable, but only in the same sense in which scarcity is undesirable; in neither case does this mean that we can avoid it. It is one of the unpleasant facts of life that certain capacities (and also certain advantages and traditions of particular organizations) cannot be duplicated, as it is a fact that certain goods are scarce. It does not make sense to disregard this fact and to attempt to create conditions "as if" competition were effective. The law cannot effectively prohibit states of affairs but only kinds of action. All we can hope for is that, whenever the possibility of competition again appears, nobody will be prevented from taking advantage of it. Where monopoly rests on man-made obstacles to entry into a market, there is every case for removing them. There is also a strong case for prohibiting price discrimination so far as is possible by the application of general rules. But the

record of governments in this field is so deplorable that it is astounding that anyone should still expect that giving governments discretionary powers will do anything but increase those obstacles. It has been the experience of all countries that discretionary powers in the treatment of monopoly are soon used to distinguish between "good" and "bad" monopolies and that authority soon becomes more concerned with protecting the supposedly good than with preventing the bad. I doubt whether there are any "good" monopolies that deserve protection. But there will always be inevitable monopolies whose transitory and temporary character is often turned into a permanent one by the solicitude of government' (pp. 265–6).

I do not think it possible to deal with the perplexities of this problem with a surer touch than is shown here.

It is time to draw to a close. I have devoted much space to displaying what seem to me to be the defects in Hayek's exposition. But they are small by the side of his achievement. He has attempted a monumental task and has inevitably fallen short of perfection. But he has left the deep impress of his mind upon his subject. No future discussion of liberty can proceed without the marks of his influence.

HARRY BURROWS ACTON

Born in London, 1908. Demy of Magdalen College, Oxford, 1927–31. Lectured on philosophy at the University College of Swansea and at Bedford College, London, 1931–40. Ministry of Supply and Board of Trade, 1940–5. Professor of Philosophy at Bedford College, University of London, 1945 onwards. Visiting Professor of Philosophy, University of Chicago, 1949. President of the Aristotelian Society, 1952–3. Editor of *Philosophy*, 1956 onwards. Author of articles in *Mind*, *Proceedings of the Aristotelian Society*, *Philosophy*, etc., and of *The Illusion of the Epoch: Marxism-Leninism as a Philosophical Creed*, 1955 (an historical and analytical examination of the Marxist-Leninist epistemology, logic, ethics and social theory). In 1959 gave the Dawes Hicks Lecture at the British Academy, published in the *Proceedings* and separately with the title *The Philosophy of Language in Revolutionary France*, 1960.

IV

Objectives

H. B. ACTON

The good society

DURING the last thirty years there has been little to encourage serious thought about the fundamentals of politics. The increasing specialisation of university studies has been against it, and a code of academic manners has grown up which sanctions no more than an ironical profession of ignorance in the face of manifest absurdities in some other person's specialism. The crisis of self-criticism and abnegation within philosophy has been against it, and philosophers have sought respectability in specialism too. But chiefly, perhaps, the course of events has been against it, since so many of the societies and institutions set up in response to the idealism of former times are foundering, and social policy is more often approached in an attitude of disillusioned pragmatism than considered in the light of principles.

Professor Hayek, in his *The Constitution of Liberty*, goes against all these tendencies. He appeals deliberately to first principles. Although entitled as few others to do so, he lays no claim to specialist expertise, and does not allow opponents to escape criticism by that device. He attempts to work out a comprehensive and closely reasoned political philosophy on the scale that our more confident predecessors found acceptable. His account of the task of the political philosopher reveals what Hayek is aiming at. It is the duty of the political philosopher, he says,

> 'to show possibilities and consequences of common action, to offer comprehensive aims of policy as a whole which the majority have not yet thought of. It is only after such a comprehensive picture of the possible results of different policies has been presented that democracy can decide what it wants' (p. 114).

The political philosopher, he goes on, should not confine himself to pointing out possibilities, but should be 'prepared to defend values which seem right to him' (p. 115), and to be critical of prevailing or majority views. Indeed, it follows from what Hayek says that the formulation of comprehensive political philosophies is essential to the functioning of a liberal-democratic society, and its absence is a sign that liberal democracy is in danger or in decline.

Aims of policy

Let us first consider, then, the comprehensive aims of policy that Hayek recommends. There is at any rate a superficial paradox in this very enterprise. For on the one hand the type of liberalism which Hayek supports is opposed to the manufacture of detailed blueprints as guides to deliberate social reconstruction, and yet on the other hand he advocates, as we have seen, the formulation of comprehensive aims of policy. But there is no real contradiction here, since Hayek rejects what he calls the rationalistic method of consciously reconstructing society, in favour of the spontaneous adjustment of free activities to one another through market processes. His view is that the arrangements and institutions that arise in this way are generally superior to those which are planned by powerful individuals or groups, however wise they may be. Various reasons are offered, but the most important is that any man or group of men must be ignorant of many of the circumstances and consequences of their policies, whereas the adjustments of a multitude of individuals to one another frequently achieve a harmony too complicated for individual comprehension. In this connection Hayek writes of 'that higher, superindividual wisdom which, in a certain sense, the products of social growth may possess' (p. 110). This is in the tradition of Bastiat, whose *Harmonies Économiques* has on its title-page the motto 'mens agitat molem'. For Hayek, as for Bastiat, the mind which works through the whole ('unites and mingles with the mighty mass', as Dryden translates it) achieves an impersonal and natural, rather than an artificial form of organisation.

Hayek contrasts his conception of a society which develops in unforeseeable ways by means of the progressive adaptation of free activities one to another, with that of a society in which an overall system of priorities is maintained by the threat of force. The latter type is most favoured today, although some of its supporters fail to realise the extent to which coercion is essential to it. In his role of critical political philosopher, therefore, Hayek reveals the bludgeon hidden behind the backs of many of those who call for social justice, fair shares, abolition of inequalities, and the like. From his criticism it emerges that in the society he would like to see, individual freedom, in the sense of freedom from coercion by the will of other men, would be taken as the guiding aim. This, however, is the least exclusive absolute that there could be, since adherence to it is the means of allowing the pursuit of many varying and conflicting ideals. The objective is, so to speak, that no objective should crowd out others, but that the way should always be left open for new ones to be invented and pursued. Hayek conceives progress not in terms of the degree of approach towards some already understood ideal, but in terms of the possibility of ideals not yet conceived. Progress, understood in this way, is a consequence of freedom.

The conditions of freedom

A free and progressive society, therefore, cannot be confined within the range of moral vision of any single man or group or class or generation. Its policies and institutions will develop and adapt themselves in unforeseeable ways. Nevertheless, there are, Hayek believes, a number of institutions and rules which, as far as can be seen at present, are essential for the preservation of any free society. Among these, private property and the rule of law are the most important. An individual is free, according to Hayek, to the extent that he is not coerced by others.* To be coerced by others is to have one's actions controlled by the will of someone else under threat of some penalty if one disobeys. The only sure way of being free is to have a private sphere into which no one else can penetrate without permission. Private property is the chief though not the sole means by which this independence is secured. It has to be maintained, of course, by the threat of governmental coercion against thieves and cheats, but the coercion is for upholding rules, not for furthering the particular aims of the property owners. A system of private property

* Discussion of Hayek's definition of freedom is not part of my assignment in this volume. I should say, however, that I agree with him that freedom, in the social and political context, is best regarded as the absence of deliberate coercion. Deliberate coercion can operate, however, indirectly as well as directly, and be exerted both by governments and by economic organisations.

established in the interests of specific persons, and varied to suit their demands, would infringe individual freedom, since those not so benefited would be coerced in the interests of the favoured owners and hence would not be free. Governmental coercion should always be in order to uphold rules. A law should not relate to specific individuals or interests, but should leave citizens free to decide which among them are to come within its scope. In this way, the coercion that is inseparable from legal enactment is kept to a minimum, and each individual can decide upon his own course of action without fear of unforeseen irruptions from the public authorities. He has quite enough to do in coping with the unpredictable effects of free activities.

The role of independence

In the society that Professor Hayek would like to see there would be a considerable proportion of people able to support themselves otherwise than by earning wages and salaries. For employed men generally are not in a position to understand the conditions in which inventiveness can flourish, so that a democracy of wage-earners will tend to favour a rather unimaginative social order. Furthermore, if there is to be freedom and progress, there must not only be opportunities but also individuals who will make opportunities for themselves and exploit them to the full. Claims to opportunities as of right are claims that people should be placed in positions guaranteed by the state, and the state can only guarantee these positions if it maintains them by force. No doubt there is a place in Hayek's vision for unambitious public service, but he makes much more of the need for active enterprise and resourcefulness. In so far as we try to find scope for our abilities, we are 'all', he remarks, 'entrepreneurs' (p. 81). No free society, Hayek argues, can make distributive justice its aim, that is distribution of incomes in accordance with merit, without putting the distribution under the control of public authorities and losing freedom thereby. The pursuit of distributive justice must, he holds, lead to an hierarchical society in which the rule of law is constantly flouted in the vain attempt to make each reward fit each individual degree of merit.*

Other contributors to this volume will discuss the application of this view of society to specific problems. There are three main topics, however, which need to be considered on a fairly abstract level. The

* I state the argument in more detail on pp. 78 ff. below.

first of these is Hayek's view about the relevance of knowledge and ignorance to social reform. His views on this matter run counter to the widely held opinion that the accumulation of knowledge and the application of scientific methods may be expected to bring social processes under conscious control for the general good.* The second main topic is that of progress. Hayek's appeal on behalf of individual freedom differs from the fashionable Existentialist protests against regimentation in that it is associated with a belief in progress rather than with a denial of its possibility.† The third topic which I propose to discuss is that of distributive justice. This is the central objective of democratic socialism, and although Hayek may be right in his view that this form of socialism is in decline, the ideal that inspires it continues to influence both popular beliefs and public policy. Discussion of it, therefore, is of practical as well as theoretical interest.

Freedom, knowledge and ignorance

Hayek holds that the fact of necessary or inevitable ignorance (he uses both adjectives) provides the chief reason for allowing the fullest possible scope to individual freedom. It is because of this ignorance that it is better to allow society to develop by spontaneous adjustment than to control it all by some central agency. Those who recognise the inevitability of ignorance will not pin their hopes on plans for society as a whole, but will want there to be scope for everyone to gain from the impersonal beneficence of transactions that are imperfectly understood. What is this inevitable ignorance, then, how does it tell in favour of limiting governmental activity, and how does it come about that a spontaneously developing society is better than one that is regulated from above?

Hayek calls attention to various types of inevitable ignorance. It is obvious how limited the knowledge of each more or less specialised individual must be. Even of the knowledge he has a considerable part is not apparent to him, since it is in the form of skills, traditions and institutions which he takes for granted. The man of science is ignorant, not only of other specialisms, but also of the unforeseeable new problems to which every scientific advance will give rise. Hayek appears to hold that these new problems are both

* John Dewey was the ablest modern supporter of this view, which, of course, goes back to Francis Bacon.

† For an Existentialist view see Karl Jaspers, *The Origin and Goal of History*, London, 1953.

theoretical (i.e. within the particular science) and practical (i.e. relative to its social effects), and that they accumulate at a faster rate than new knowledge does. If this is so, then the hope, entertained by so many since the time of the Enlightenment, of a gradual diminution in the field of ignorance, is seen to be illusory. Again, people do not know what they really want until specimen opportunities have come to their notice. Still less, therefore, can anyone know what future generations will want. From all this it follows, in Hayek's view, that the men who would be called upon to devise and implement a comprehensive social plan cannot possibly know enough for their project to be a reasonable one. The likelihood is that it will misfire, prove unsatisfactory to those for whom it is devised, give rise to all sorts of unforeseen reactions, and ultimately appear pointless in the light of future systems of valuation.

This view raises philosophical questions of great interest which we must reluctantly ignore. I confess that I do not follow Hayek's argument for the view that growth in scientific knowledge constantly extends the field of ignorance. It is rather misleading, I suggest, to call the opening up of new and unsolved problems a growth of the realm of ignorance. It is rather the replacing of mere ignorance or nescience, i.e. complete unawareness that there is anything to be known, by a set of unanswered questions hitherto not conceived of. Blank nescience becomes specific ignorance with more blank nescience beyond it. Although this renders untenable the idea that knowledge can ever be completed, it does not appear in itself to provide a reason against comprehensive social plans based on whatever scientific knowledge is available.

However, the main element in the argument from ignorance is that no one can know enough about how men's wants can be satisfied, and about what men's future wants will be, to justify embarking on comprehensive governmental plans for their satisfaction. Hayek does not discuss the point, but it would appear that governments have means of collecting and collating knowledge which private individuals do not have. It must be his view, then, that the advantage that governments have in this respect is not enough to justify their claiming to have the knowledge necessary for their plans. Such knowledge would have to be so vast as to be outside the comprehension of any man or group or organisation. But how can we be so sure that this is the case? I do not think that Hayek's thesis is based on any calculation of more or less. It is rather an implication of some propositions about predictability. Certain actions and certain wants, on this view, are unpredictable. It is not known how other people will react except in so far as they follow routines. Resourcefulness and inventiveness can, in general, be expected from some people, but the forms which they will take are so various that they cannot be anticipated in any central plan. Furthermore, people do not in general know what they want until they get it. New wants are frequently the result of some accidental encounter, and no one can predict what will arouse them. The planner's task is impossible because if he is to succeed he must foresee the unforeseeable.

I am myself convinced that the argument from unpredictability is a strong one. Its force, nevertheless, would be somewhat lessened in a society where ingenuity was rare, science stagnant and wants stereotyped. If it were possible to utilise electronic computers in planning for such societies, then the range of predictability could be extended. A society can for a time, perhaps for a long time, be rendered *more* predictable by being strait-jacketed. It is in the free and progressive societies that Hayek so eloquently depicts that unpredictability is, so to say, endemic. On this matter he speaks, I think, with two voices in the space of one page. On the one hand he suggests that if there were omniscient men 'there would be little case for liberty' (p. 29). On the other hand he holds that 'Liberty is essential in order to leave room for the unforeseeable and unpredictable' and to allow scope for 'the emergence of what we shall want when we see it' (p. 29). It might be argued that there is no conflict here, that Hayek, in saying there would be little case for liberty if there were omniscient men, is not weakening his argument at all since it is, as he says, 'the main contention' (p. 29) of his view that there are not and could not be omniscient men. But when he argues that liberty serves the purpose of leaving room for the unforeseeable and unpredictable, he is resting his case, not on the *impossibility* of there being knowledge that leads to successful social planning, but on the *undesirability* of a society in which coercively imposed planning prevents the development of the unexpected. If the unexpected and unpredictable are necessary anyway, why is freedom required in order to leave room for them? Hayek thinks, and I agree with him, that a society in which room is kept open for novelty and invention is better than one of enforced routines.

Free societies deliberately lay themselves open to the inspirations provided by the new and unexpected. Hence they will, by their variety and inventiveness, actively prevent the possibility of anything approaching social omniscience. Omniscient men are only conceivable, if at all, in societies where routine prevails, in the sort of society favoured by Mr. Khrushchev, in which 'every minute is calculated, a life built on calculation.*' It is not that liberty would be unnecessary if there were omniscient men, but that men who prize liberty will develop their knowledge, their aims and their skills so that social omniscience is rendered impossible.

The spontaneously developing society that Hayek advocates is one in which individuals and associations make arrangements with one another within a framework of criminal and civil law. Each individual and each group will act in the light of the knowledge relevant to its own concerns – and these need not, of course, be selfish. If A and B come to a certain agreement, this will have repercussions for C and D who, in their turn, will adapt themselves in the ways that seem best to them. In this way an interlocking system of adjustments will arise of enormous extent and complexity. The whole that emerges from this is not the best conceivable, for there is no comprehensive view of it. But it will be more free than the alternative form of order because fewer possibilities of action will be forcibly excluded or kept from being thought of.

Progress

Progress may be regarded as advance towards some definitely determined goal, or as a movement in which new goals are constantly emerging. Professor Hayek is mainly concerned with progress of this second sort. From what has already been said, it will be seen that according to Hayek progress of this sort is a consequence of freedom, on the ground that when scope is given to spontaneous activity, chance and experiment elicit hitherto unconceived aims and preferences. The growth of the sciences is progressive in this way, as application to one set of problems opens the road to further problems only conceivable on the basis of the solutions found to the first. Comparable developments take place in the growth of technique, of tastes and perhaps of institutions. Hayek is particularly

* *New York Times*, 2nd March, 1960, quoted in *Problems of Communism*, Vol. IX, No. 6, p. 10.

impressed by the progressive development of wants, since this means that future generations will have other scales of preference than our own. He extends this idea to moral codes. Moral rules are not deliberately framed, and a new system of them could never be constructed all at once. Nevertheless, he speaks of their being modified and improved under the impulsion of experience (p. 63). But this idea, I think, needs very careful examination if liberalism (or, as Hayek prefers to call it, 'libertarianism') is not to collapse into moral nihilism. Indeed, this, in my view, is the danger to which liberalism, in the twentieth century, is most liable to succumb – the danger of indiscriminate tolerance.

In order to bring out its weakness we need to distinguish, I think, between primary and secondary moral rules. A primary moral rule is universal and irremovable. Once acknowledged as part of the corpus of morality, its exclusion, although theoretically conceivable, is morally unthinkable. For example, the rules prohibiting cruelty and false witness are just not subjects for moral reform. On the other hand, there are more specific moral rules such as some of those relating to property or to sexual behaviour, which can be modified without affecting the primary ones. It is these secondary ones that permit of moral innovation, experimentation and development, whereas the primary ones are not of a type that allows this. (The principle enunciated by Aquinas that the primary principles allow additions but no removals is in my view correct.) What I have called primary moral principles coincide with what was formerly called the natural law. This doctrine, in its earlier formulations, cannot be easily accommodated to present-day modes of thought, but without it liberalism would not have been created and would not long survive. There is an essential conservatism about morals which is lacking from natural science, where no principles (apart perhaps from principles of method) are irremovable. It was at one time a task of liberalism to secure freedom for the pursuit of natural science, but liberalism commits suicide if it takes the sort of progress characteristic of natural science as generally operative. If we compare the additive progress of the moral law with the transformative progress of the natural sciences we see that within the various departments of human life there are different sorts of progress. Thus the progress of society as a whole must remain an elusive idea, if, indeed, it has any meaning at all.

I am suggesting, then, that the development of morality should not be assimilated to the progress of science, that there are aspects of morality that, once appreciated, permit of specification but not of abolition. I suggest, furthermore, that it is a defect of contemporary liberalism that it does not unambiguously recognise this. A consequence of not recognising it is to introduce into the liberal outlook a form of moral scepticism which could well prove fatal. By comparison with the systems opposed to it, liberalism is, of course, critical and undogmatic, but no outlook can survive at all if it regards *all* rules of behaviour as merely provisional. There is nothing self-stultifying in holding that the science and art of the distant future may take forms that are now unimaginable to us, but seriously to suppose that this could hold for morality (or for logic) opens the way to nihilism.

Hayek is far from being a nihilist, for it is a leading feature of his book that in it liberalism is defended, as Constant put it, as the 'system of principles'. Nevertheless, I do not think that he altogether avoids the difficulties inherent in regarding progress as a single concept. He appears to think that if progress is towards what is not yet known it cannot be justified in terms of its end. In one passage he therefore seems to justify it in terms of movement. 'Progress', he writes, 'is movement for movement's sake' (p. 41). If this stood alone it would be most unconvincing, for why should some people not prefer to stand still? Hayek also says, however, that human intelligence 'proves itself' by 'living in and for the future' (p. 41), and that 'it is in the process of learning and in the effects of having learned something new, that man enjoys the gift of his intelligence' (p. 41). These phrases imply that the movement that is for movement's sake is the exercise of intelligence in invention and discovery – an exercise, he points out, from which the less intelligent get benefits (pp. 41–2). It would seem that scientific discovery and technological invention are being put forward as intrinsically valuable for those who engage in them and as means to the happiness of those who do not. If this is what Hayek means, then he is regarding the advance of science as the aim and justification of progress.

Distributive justice

According to Hayek, 'distributive justice is irreconcilable with freedom in the choice of one's activities: it is the justice of a hierarchic organisation, not of a free society' (p. 440). By 'distributive justice' he means distribution of rewards in accordance with merit, and by 'merit' he means 'the attributes of conduct that make it deserving of praise, that is, the moral character of the action, and not the value of the achievement' (p. 94). By 'value of the achievement' he means, I think, what the beneficiaries of the achievement are prepared freely to pay for it. He objects to distribution in accordance with merit in the first place because there is no objective means of assessing it. When the attempt is made, distribution can be decided only in accordance with what other people decide it is. When the reward is determined in terms of the work or product offered the transaction is between two willing parties, whereas when it is determined by assessing the merit of the producer, this can only be decided by some public body. Distribution in accordance with value needs no authority to determine it, but only to keep the parties from coercing one another. Distribution in accordance with merit can only be secured by a public assessment and enforcement of who merits how much. Furthermore, once this sort of distribution is established in respect of one type of income, it will be demanded in respect of more and more until all incomes are decided on the basis of a publicly established scale of merit. Hayek contrasts this system, which assumes a single set of moral priorities, with the system he prefers, in which people's dealings by way of service and exchange are largely independent of the moral outlooks of the parties involved.

My first comment is that it would have been better if Hayek had written of distribution in accordance with *desert* rather than in accordance with merit. When desert is taken as the measure, it becomes obvious that it is associated with demerit as well as with merit, with punishment as well as with reward. Hence to call for distribution in these moral terms is to call for a society in which, under official auspices, men are constantly rehearsing a travesty of the Day of Judgment. This would certainly require a respect for the authorities and a degree of regimentation greater even than was found in Calvin's Geneva.

But distributive justice is seldom conceived in such strict terms. More often the argument is that remuneration should be justified in terms of the skill, training and moral qualities required for the job. It seems to me that remuneration in accordance with such qualities may be influenced by custom, which is impersonal like the market, and like market prices is not ordained. If this is so, then a customary but uncoercive hierarchy is a third possibility between a coercive hierarchy (Herbert Spencer's 'militant type of society') on the one hand and a society based on uncoerced agreements (Spencer's 'industrial type of society') on the other.* Hayek's most powerful objection to distribution in accordance with merit is not, then, that it requires force to maintain it (it often does, of course), but that it ignores commutative justice. For distribution in accordance with merit is from the point of view of the worker and ignores the requirements of the user of his product. The producer's moral claims must be met before there is any question of the consumer's wishes. This can lead to demands for payment for work that is not required on the ground that skill and effort have been put into it. On moral grounds someone would be having to pay for what he does not get. One sort of justice would be driving out the other.

It is clear that an equal distribution of incomes would conflict with a distribution in accordance with desert, and in fact few have advocated it. Nevertheless, over the past one hundred years there has been an increasing pressure *towards* equality. Hayek is not averse to this in principle.

> 'One may well feel attracted' [he writes], 'to a community in which there are no extreme contrasts between rich and poor and may welcome the fact that the general increase in wealth seems gradually to reduce those differences. I fully share these feelings and certainly regard the degree of social equality that the United States has achieved as wholly admirable' (pp. 87–88).

His objection to egalitarianism is (briefly) that it requires the granting of excessive power to men who cannot know enough to use it properly. Furthermore, equal distribution would hinder the development of capacities which are of advantage in the first place to the individuals who profit by them, but in the long run to all the other members of the community.

Hayek does not, however, directly consider an aspect of egalitarianism which is widely accepted today, the view that justice requires any distribution to be equal unless there are reasons to the contrary. If it is accepted that the presumption is in favour of equality and that the burden of proof is on those who would depart from it, then existing unequal states of affairs are put on the de-

* *The Principles of Sociology*, Vol. II (1882), pp. 658–730.

fensive as against an ideal equality. It is necessary, therefore, to comment briefly on this fundamentally radical view.

Support for it, I believe, is partly due to the fact that equality is a feature of any distribution in accordance with rules.* It is of the essence of a rule that similar cases are dealt with in a similar way. For example, if there is a rule of distribution such that payment is in proportion to output, then the rule is violated if men whose output is the same do not get the same reward. What has been called 'formal justice' is achieved when all the members of a given category are treated in the same way.† If the rule of distribution were in proportion to height or weight formal justice would be secured so long as men of the same height or weight obtained the same reward. A distribution that was not in accordance with formal justice would be whimsical, arbitrary or irregular.

Upholders of the view I am considering, however, would want substantial as well as mere formal equality. One line of argument is that everyone has an equal right to consideration or respect and that any departure from equal treatment would violate this right unless there were adequate reasons for it. It seems to me, however, that the right to consideration or respect is absolute and that no violation of it could be justified by any reason whatsoever. Is a man not being treated with respect if he receives less than someone else who is in like case with himself? I think he is not if he is in this position as a result of deliberate arrangements, as he would be, for example, if he were employed by the same employer on the same work. To employ several people for similar work, and to pay less to some than to others, and yet to have no justification for this on grounds of time or effort or output or seniority or exhaustion of funds or some other reason, leaves lack of respect or downright contempt as the only alternatives. (In a free market, of course, the aggrieved man could go elsewhere.) But differences of reward that are not deliberately contrived are quite different. For A is not failing to respect B merely because R is paying S more than A is paying B. If this is denied, then the assumption is being made that it is wrong to *allow* different systems of reward to exist side by side. This, in its turn, implies that the attempt should be made to bring all systems of reward under deliberate and co-ordinated control. These steps, I believe, give support to

* Sir Isaiah Berlin, 'Equality', *Proceedings of the Aristotelian Society*, 1955–6, p. 305.

† Ch. Perelman, *De la Justice*, Brussels, 1945, p. 27.

Hayek's view that the pursuit of distributive justice tends to become *total*, and does this not only in practice, but as a matter of logic.

Another aim of those who strive for distributive justice (or social justice, as they more often call it) is to break down the divisions between classes. The argument here, I think, is not merely that the class structure prevents the distribution of incomes from being equal or in accordance with merit, but also that in the absence of class distinctions men would associate with one another more easily and with greater friendliness than they do now.* Briefly, the point is that if greater social equality is brought about by governmental measures, the result will be an increase in fraternity. It is, of course, most hazardous to prophesy the moral effects of political changes, and it is open to doubt whether a spread of friendly feeling could be secured in such a way. But Professor Hayek, I think, is less perturbed by the absence of universal brotherhood than some socialists would think he ought to be. At any rate he calls attention to the fact that the workings of the market enable men freely to benefit one another even though they do not share the same tastes or moral outlook. I think he regards it as an advantage that business arrangements are separable from personal attachments. In a society where men are free to choose their friends, there are bound to be groups which disapprove of one another. This should not prevent their respecting one another's rights, but they are not required to seek for friendship with those they find uncongenial. Absurd class distinctions are better dealt with by ridicule than by legislation.

Conclusion

Professor Hayek's main theses depend on the distinction between the essential features of free association on the one hand and enforced hierarchy on the other. Free association requires the maintenance by force of private property and the rule of law. A society where free association predominates will be complex, morally variegated and unpredictably progressive. Those who seek to bring society under centralised control necessarily extend the area of coercion, impose a single moral scheme, and diminish the possibilities of progress. Furthermore, when their plan is devised to secure distributive justice, incomes are settled and enforced so as to maintain an hierarchical order in which little attention is given to a man's right to

* C. A. R. Crosland, *The Future of Socialism*, 1956, p. 169.

pay for what he wants; what he has to pay for is the cost of upholding the status of the suppliers.

The contrast between free association and coercive hierarchy is, of course, a contrast of ideal types, and in actual societies the two elements are found in varying proportions. But Hayek is doing an important service in calling attention once more to the enormous difference between being assigned a place and making an agreement. Contract has certain moral advantages over status which at present tend to be lost sight of. Perhaps I have stressed more than Hayek has done the moral difference between these types of social order. I have in mind particularly two observations by Adam Smith in *The Wealth of Nations*, Book I, Chapter II. The first is that 'It is not from the benevolence of the butcher, the brewer, or the baker that we expect our dinner . . .', and the second is that 'when an animal wants to obtain something either of a man or of another animal it has no other means of persuasion but to gain the favour of those whose services it requires', and that some men too who want things from their fellows endeavour 'by every servile and fawning attention to obtain their good will'. Adam Smith contrasts with this the method of offering something in exchange for what is desired. This is the method of independent men who can co-operate without servility and without more than a minimum of moral agreement. This type of arrangement allows moral differences to co-exist with social cohesion. If men will only do business with those whose ideals they share, society is faced with the alternatives of uniformity or disruption. The boycott is not necessarily a sign of enhanced moral sensibility.

At this point I must mention a possible objection to Hayek's view which should not be allowed to pass unnoticed. He argues on the one hand that, because of their inevitable ignorance, planners are bound to fail in their attempts to build a society that conforms to their ideals. On the other hand he argues that the future of free societies is likewise unpredictable. Now an objector may well ask what reason there can be for preferring one unpredictability to another. The answer must be that the unpredictability of the coercive social order is linked with the failure of coercion and hence with the likelihood of social breakdown and civil strife, whereas the unpredictability of the (relatively) non-coercive social order relates to the positive discoveries and arrangements by which men adjust their relations to one another. The unforeseen consequences of coercion, it would seem, are more likely to be bad than are the unforeseen possibilities left open in a free society. A further point is that the failure of coercive plans is not completely unforeseen, although the planners themselves do not foresee it. On the other hand, many of the future achievements of a free society are absolutely unpredictable, for the reasons which have already been given.

As I see it, then, Professor Hayek's main theme is the contrast between the form of organisation that arises out of agreements freely entered into and the form that is forcibly imposed by some central authority. I agree that this is a most important distinction, though I do not think that Hayek pays sufficient attention to the fact that hierarchy and status can arise without being forcibly imposed by anyone. He goes on to argue that those who value freedom will prefer the first form of order, and will try to confine the second form to the work of upholding the first. With this, which was Locke's view, no liberal, it seems to me, can disagree. Hayek justifies his preference for the first form of order by the argument that no one can know enough to make the predictions necessary for operating the second sort effectively, and by the argument that freedom is best secured by leaving room for the unforeseeable. I find it logically disconcerting when social predictions are regarded both as impossible and as undesirable, for there would be no point in urging the prevention of the impossible. I have therefore suggested that social predictions are likely to be more successful in strait-jacketed societies than in societies where invention is encouraged. I have also suggested that Hayek, in regarding freedom as the basis for progress considered as single and total, inadvertently encourages the nihilism that is the Achilles' heel of liberalism. In my view Hayek succeeds in showing that when distributive justice is made the object of public policy a forcibly imposed hierarchy has to be set up. But I do not think that he considers all, or even the most important, of the arguments for the general establishment of a system of distributive justice. I believe, however, that they can be dealt with within the framework of his view, in which commutative justice – which is logically linked with the first form of order – receives its rightful emphasis. That there is indeed a logical link between free association and distributive justice, and a certain incompatibility between free association and a universally imposed distributive justice, is one of the most interesting conclusions of this most penetrating book.

PART TWO

Policy in a Free Society

E. VICTOR MORGAN

Born at Horbury, Warwickshire, 1915. Educated Warwick School and Sidney Sussex College, Cambridge; post-graduate student, Christ's College, Cambridge, 1938–41. Went to Swansea, 1941, as temporary assistant lecturer and stayed. Appointed to chair of economics, 1945. Rockefeller travelling fellowship in U.S.A., 1949–50. Visiting professor, Columbia University, summer sessions 1953 and 1957. Main research interests are in the development of monetary and financial institutions and in monetary policy. Author of *The Theory and Practice of Central Banking, 1797–1913*, *Conquest of Unemployment*, *Studies in British Financial Policy, 1914–25*, *A First Approach to Economics*, *The Structure of Property Ownership in Great Britain*, etc.

V

The Monetary Framework

E. VICTOR MORGAN

Introduction

PROFESSOR HAYEK shows good reasons for believing that no society can long remain free if it fails to maintain a reasonably stable monetary system, but he also recognises that money is an exception to the general rule of relying upon a free market. As Sir Robert Peel said in moving the Bank Charter Act of 1844, the virtue of free competition is to produce the greatest supply at the lowest price and 'we do not want an abundant supply of cheap promissory paper'.

Hayek traces this exceptional position of money to three circumstances of varying degrees of generality and validity. First and most general is the cumulative movements that arise from the interdependence of income and expenditure; an 'autonomous' rise in spending in one section of the economy will lead to increased incomes and so to 'induced' increases in spending elsewhere; so long as the primary, autonomous rise in spending continues, the induced rise will continue also, but if the form of spending which had initially increased falls back to its original level, the flow of income and of induced spending will be reversed. These relationships are the heart of most modern theories of economic fluctuations. Hayek links them directly with changes in the money supply through the fact that 'money, unlike ordinary commodities, serves not by being used up but by being handed on' (p. 325). Not all economists would accept the link in this form, but nearly all would agree that the income-expenditure relationships in an industrial economy create fluctuations which need a controlled money supply as a regulator.

Secondly, when a large part of the money stock consists of bank credit, there may be times at which an uncontrolled system would produce a 'perversely elastic' supply of money. Circumstances (e.g. the fear of a financial crisis or the threat of political disturbance) which made the public want to hold more money could also make the banks want to lend less, and vice versa. These two characteristics of money have led to the growth or creation of central banks with a general responsibility for the regulation of credit and for acting as 'lender of last resort'. A third, the large volume of government payments and government debts in modern states, has led to a very close association between central banks and treasuries. This condition is obviously less general than the other two but it nevertheless must be taken as given in most of the near-free societies of today. Even if the present level of expenditure were substantially reduced, government payments would still be very large in relation to the other transactions of the money market.

The close association between central banks and governments raises special problems in the fight against inflation. Here Hayek sees a vicious circle: the welfare state creates strong inflationary pressures through its high level of public expenditure and its commitment to maintain 'full employment'; and inflation leads to further extensions of state activity by impairing the working of the free market, and by making it more difficult for individuals to provide their own protection against old age or misfortune through saving. This process can only be halted if the same politicians whose employment and expenditure policies are creating inflation can be induced to resist it in their monetary policies. At the worst this could involve an impossible set of contradictions: at best it calls for much strength of mind.

The menace to freedom is, for Hayek, the greatest evil of inflation but it is by no means the only one. Large changes in the value of money cause arbitrary redistributions of wealth and are a breach of faith with all who have long-term contracts expressed in money. Fluctuations in the unit of account make rational calculation impossible, especially in the field of investment, and so impair the working of the market. These arguments would apply equally to deflation, but Hayek contends that deflation is less to be feared since its evils are more obvious and, in present-day societies, likely to create immediate political pressures for countervailing action. Inflation, particularly when combined with very high tax rates on large personal incomes, and on business profits, discourages saving, encourages the taking of short rather than long views and, by giving an artificial stimulus to investment while it lasts, creates a maldistribution of resources and makes it more difficult to avoid eventual deflation. Thus Hayek would argue that, contrary to widely held beliefs, inflation retards rather than accelerates long-run economic progress.

A logical consequence of these views might seem to be that monetary authorities should be made independent of governments and bound by rigid rules that would force them to resist inflation. Here, however, Hayek finds himself obliged to temper logic with judgment of what is practicable. Thus he regards a return to the gold standard as impracticable and, in any case, of doubtful use, as the value of gold would be unduly influenced by the policies of a few large countries. He is sympathetic towards a commodity reserve standard, designed to stabilise the average price of a large number of commodities, but sees no great hope of its adoption. Moreover, even when a standard is laid down by rule, central banks have to exercise a good deal of discretion in shaping detailed policies to conform with the general rule. For reasons already mentioned he doubts whether central banks can be made truly independent of governments. He concludes, therefore, that it is better to prescribe objectives of monetary policy than to lay down rigid rules governing the conduct of monetary institutions and their relations with the government. The fundamental reason why governments have allowed inflation to persist is that they have regarded 'full employment' as a more important objective than price stability; Hayek concludes emphatically that these priorities should be reversed, and that if this were done, price stability could be maintained without creating serious unemployment. There can be little doubt of the validity of the first part of this argument; the second depends to some extent on changes in the attitudes, power and legal status of the trade unions.

Objectives of monetary policy

In his plea that price stability should be made the primary objective of policy, Professor Hayek states that

> 'During the two hundred years preceding 1914 when Great Britain adhered to the gold standard, the price level, so far as it can be

> meaningfully measured over such a period, fluctuated around a constant level ending up pretty well where it started and rarely changing by more than a third above or below that average level (except during the period of the Napoleonic Wars, when the gold standard was abandoned)' (p. 329).

There is no doubt of the literal truth of this statement, but the manner in which it is put tends to minimise the extent of fluctuations. Anyone wishing to draw attention to the fluctuations rather than the stability could point out that a change from one-third above to one-third below an average implies a fall of 50 per cent, or a peak (133 based on the average as 100) twice as high as the trough (66). There were, in fact, fluctuations of this order of magnitude extending over periods of twenty to thirty years during the eighteenth and nineteenth centuries. No completely satisfactory explanation of these changes has yet been found, but they appear to have been associated with changes in the balance between the world supply of and demand for gold. Within these long periods of slowly rising or slowly falling prices there were also quite sharp, though brief, fluctuations which were associated with those changes in employment and business activity generally known as the trade cycle. So far as both these types of fluctuation are concerned a modern monetary system should be able to do better than the eighteenth and nineteenth century gold standard. A currency which is not rigidly linked to gold need not be affected by fluctuations in the value of that metal which appear to have caused the long waves of inflation and deflation in the past. We have also learnt a lot about the mechanism of the trade cycle, and, since short-period fluctuations in prices were closely linked with fluctuations in employment, policies which stabilise the one should also help to stabilise the other. It is in this sense that Hayek rightly maintains that there is no necessary inconsistency between stability in prices and in employment.

Both these types of price fluctuation are, however, very different from the inflation that has plagued Britain and a large part of the Western world since 1945. This has been associated with a high level of government expenditure (both on social services and on armaments), 'full employment', and an unlimited supply of paper money, a combination of circumstances that Britain, at least, has previously experienced only in wartime.

The government commitment to maintain full employment has

been interpreted not only as providing greater stability, but also a much higher average level of employment than in the past. During the second half of the nineteenth century, unemployment among trade unionists ranged from about 2 per cent in the boom to about 10 per cent in depression. Figures for other workers are not known but, since they were largely unskilled, their average level of unemployment was probably rather higher, and the range of fluctuations at least as great. By contrast, in post-war Britain unemployment has varied between about 1 per cent and 2 per cent of the whole employed population. This high level of employment of labour has generally been matched by a very high rate of utilisation of industrial plant, and by bulging order books and long delivery dates.

This running of the economy at maximum capacity has been defended both as avoiding the waste and the social evils of unemployment, and in the belief that it is conducive to a high rate of growth. This, however, is almost certainly a delusion. Apart from creating a constant danger of inflation there are many disadvantages in too high a level of activity; it leads to waste of resources through 'bottlenecks'; it encourages firms to order materials and hold on to labour in excess of current need; it creates conditions in which the inefficient can survive and in which the efficient cannot get resources for expansion; and it breeds an attitude of mind both in workers and management that is far from helpful to rapid growth. A society that is content to work a little below capacity is likely to make better use of its opportunities for growth and soon to outstrip in wealth one that is constantly striving to keep all its resources in use.

This is not, of course, an argument for mass unemployment. It is, however, an argument for balancing the advantages of a high level of employment against the disadvantages of 'over-full employment'. Naturally, the evils we have mentioned grow as the economy approaches nearer and nearer to capacity, but this progression is by no means a smooth one. On the contrary, there seems to be a quite narrow range of employment which is critical; below this the diseconomies of working 'flat out' are unimportant, above it they increase very rapidly. The exact position of this critical range will depend upon many circumstances, and will vary from time to time and from place to place. The experience of post-war Britain suggests that we have generally been operating above, but not always very far above, the critical range. If unemployment fluctuated between

2 per cent and 3 per cent instead of between 1 per cent and 2 per cent (with a corresponding increase of reserve capacity in capital) it could make a very big difference both to the behaviour of prices and to the ultimate pace of economic growth.

The causes of inflation

In an economy running very near to capacity inflation can arise in several ways. Since little if any immediate increase in the total supply of goods is possible, any general increase in demand, whatever its cause, must tend to raise prices. The initial impetus may, however, come from the side of costs. A very high level of employment will enhance the power of trade unions and reduce the incentive to managements to resist wage claims. If unions in general ask for and get wage increases substantially in excess of any increase in productivity that may have occurred, employers will find their money costs increased and will recoup themselves by putting up their prices; wage-earners will, however, be receiving higher money incomes, so that an increase in demand (in terms of money) is automatically created, and the rise in prices will tend to be self-sustaining.

Another process, similar but rather more subtle, is probably commoner. This depends upon the inter-action of three beliefs deeply embedded in the trade union movement and commanding a wide measure of support outside: first, that an increase in wages is justified by an increase in productivity in the trade or industry concerned; secondly, that an increase can also be justified by a rise in the cost of living; and, thirdly, that relative wages 'ought' to be 'fair' as between different occupations, giving similar rewards for similar degrees of skill. What is regarded as 'fair' in this way is, of course, very much influenced by tradition. Suppose now that workers in an industry where there has been rapid technological progress get an increase in wages proportionate to the rise in their productivity. There will, of course, be no difficulty in paying this without any increase in the price of the commodity concerned, but these fortunate wage-earners will now have improved their position (probably through no special merit or effort of their own) in relation to others in industries where technological progress has been less rapid. Workers in these industries will then put in a claim on grounds of 'fairness' and this could not be met without raising the price of the goods which they produce. Thus some prices will remain constant and others will rise; on average the cost of living will have risen, and this will be a ground for further wage claims which, again, cannot be met without a further rise in prices.

This sort of mechanism has played an important part in post-war inflation in Britain and, probably, in most other industrial countries, and it will continue to give trouble until there is a marked change in the attitudes mentioned above. Technological progress is bound to be uneven between different industries, and this must be reflected in changes in relative prices; goods in the production of which progress is rapid become relatively cheap and those where progress is slow become relatively dear. If even the most progressive industries can only keep their prices (in absolute terms) stable, then the general level of prices must obviously rise. The general level can only be stabilised if wages in progressive industries rise less than in proportion to productivity and part of the benefit of progress is passed on (as it should be) to the consumer in the form of lower prices. This would happen automatically in a society in which competition was free and labour perfectly mobile; the movement of workers would prevent wages in any one occupation from getting out of line with those in others of similar skill and difficulty; and competition would ensure that lower costs were passed on in lower prices. Perfect mobility is obviously unattainable, but the greater is mobility and the keener is competition the easier it is to keep this sort of inflation in check.

The relationship of these processes to the money supply is complicated and, in some respects, still controversial. Clearly neither of the processes we have analysed is set in motion by a change in the money supply, so that these kinds of inflation can hardly be said to be caused by monetary influences. Equally clearly, however, higher wages and higher prices mean a larger money value of transactions, and this increase in money payments can only be met if there is an increase either in the amount of money or in the velocity of its circulation. If neither of these things could come about, then a brake would be put on, and the inflationary process would grind to a halt.

Here, however, it is necessary to make two qualifications. First, when a community holds very large amounts of short-term debt, payable either by one another or by the government, it is very difficult for the monetary authorities to apply the brake without producing a financial crisis. The British economy emerged from the war with a vast amount of short-term government debt, and attempts to reduce it have been frustrated by the high level of government expenditure and by the reluctance of the public (largely as a result of inflation) to buy long-dated government securities. This has been a major weakness in the monetary mechanism during the past few years. Secondly, if the brake were applied effectively, producers would find that they could not pass on their enhanced wage costs by selling at higher prices, production would be curtailed and unemployment would arise, and would persist until either the monetary brake was taken off again or there was a change in attitudes making possible a fall in wages. It is this type of inflation that does create an inconsistency between stability of prices and stability of employment and so poses a dilemma for governments pledged to maintain both.

The instruments of monetary policy

The basic instrument of monetary policy is, of course, the power exercised by the central bank by virtue of its twin function as bankers' bank and lender of last resort. As bankers' bank the central bank can vary the amount of its own lending and so produce variations in the cash reserve of other banks. However, the central bank's powers in this respect are limited by its obligation as lender of last resort. It is a long-standing convention, and a necessary part of the system that a central bank should never refuse to lend on good security to those entitled to deal with it. Hence if a central bank were to curtail bank reserves unduly, the banks could always replenish them by borrowing (directly or indirectly) from it. The central bank can, however, fix the rate at which it will operate as lender of last resort (known in Britain as Bank rate) and so can influence the whole pattern of interest rates and the lending policy of financial institutions. For all the criticism to which it has been exposed, Bank rate remains the most important instrument of monetary policy, with market operations (variations in the volume of central bank lending) as an important supplement.

The control over interest rates brought about by these means is entirely non-discriminatory and non-coercive – an ideal instrument, as Hayek's criteria indicate, for a free market economy. Unfortunately, however, variations in interest rates produce their full effect only over a considerable period of time, so that a lot of foresight is necessary if they are to maintain the high degree of stability that modern governments desire. Moreover, the effect of interest rates has been dulled by high taxation (since many interest charges can be deducted from income before it is assessed for tax) and by the large volume of money and very short-term debt left over by war finance. In Britain this second difficulty has been aggravated by two other features of the system. The government has had to raise so much capital for public investment that it has been unable to reduce, and has found it hard to avoid increasing, its short-term debt; and this debt is held, to a very large extent, by the banking system. To some extent inflation provides its own way out of these difficulties; the rise in output, prices and property values has meant that liquid assets are relatively less important in relation both to national income and capital than they were a few years ago. There is still, however, a need to reduce the volume of short-term debt, and this involves accepting a long-term interest rate (however high it may be) at which the public is prepared to buy long-term government bonds. It would also be desirable that more Treasury bills should be held outside the banks, and this can be encouraged by keeping market rate of discount near to Bank rate and, therefore, well above the banks' deposit rate (conventionally fixed at 2 per cent below Bank rate).

These changes could considerably increase the effectiveness of variations in interest rates but, even so, they may need to be supplemented by other measures. In considering some of those which are either in operation or which have been proposed, we are looking for measures which are non-coercive and non-discriminatory, which use the market mechanism and which are so far as possible predictable, though the last criterion is seldom likely to be very well fulfilled.*

First, there is a family of closely related measures, all of which are designed to influence the total lending of the banks by operating upon the volume of some particular asset in relation to some prescribed or conventional ratio. These would include the variable reserve ratio of the Federal Reserve System, and the 'liquidity ratio' and 'special deposits' scheme in Britain. These score quite good marks according to our criteria; they discriminate against the banks in relation to other financial institutions but not in any very harsh way; they affect only the total volume of lending, and they leave the banks free to choose the type of loan and to use market mechanisms;

* See *The Constitution of Liberty*, particularly chapters 9 and 10.

and they are as predictable as monetary measures are likely to be. Perhaps their biggest disadvantage is that some of them, such as special deposits, could be used to facilitate government borrowing and save the Treasury from the discipline of having to reduce the floating debt. Much worse, in all respects, are the official requests to banks to restrict either the total amount of their advances or their advances for particular purposes. These involve coercion of the banks and discrimination both between them and other institutions and between various classes of customer.

At first sight it might seem that the second type of pressure is more obnoxious than the first, but there is little to choose between them; even restriction on the total amount of advances involves discrimination between those who rely particularly on this form of credit and those who use other forms, e.g. bills. All forms of official request or direction of this kind are inimical to sound monetary policy and have no place in a free economy. Restrictions on hire purchase contain large elements of arbitrary discrimination both between consumers and between the producers of goods bought and not bought in this way. They have big advantages in producing a very quick effect on demand and in the fact that the industries most affected by them have often been those where demand is most outrunning productive capacity. They are, however, dangerous weapons for a free society. One other way in which the monetary authorities can make their operations both more effective and more predictable is by providing more adequate information about the nature of and the reasons for their market operations; in spite of some recent progress, the British authorities still have a long way to go in this respect.

Finally, though rather outside the subject of this essay, there are certain types of fiscal measures which can influence the rate of spending and which could give valuable support to monetary action. Among those which come out well when tested by our previous criteria are a variable social security contribution, a general sales tax and the investment allowance. Variations in taxes at the economically appropriate time raise constitutional problems, but these could be overcome if Parliament were to specify, in the annual finance act, a range for certain taxes within which the Chancellor was authorised to make variations.*

* Professor Morgan's suggestion constitutes a noteworthy anticipation of the new powers taken by the Chancellor of the Exchequer in the 1961 Budget.—Ed.

Rule and discretion in monetary policy

No monetary system can rely entirely upon rules, and the central bank must always have discretion. In the British form of the gold standard, the Bank was given only three rules – it might issue only a fixed amount of notes not covered by gold; it must buy gold at a fixed price; and it must pay its notes in legal gold coin on demand. The Bank was then left to order its affairs so as always to be able to keep these rules and at times this involved a very large element of discretion. At present the British Government is bound by one very important monetary rule, its obligation to the International Monetary Fund to maintain a stable external value of the pound except for changes that may be made within the rules of the Fund. This rule reproduces, though in a somewhat less rigid form, the external stability of the gold standard. But the gold standard also regulated the domestic supply of legal tender money, and to this regulation there is no effective counterpart today. The Currency and Banknotes Act, 1954 does prescribe a limit, but it also authorises the issue of statutory orders allowing that limit to be exceeded; a succession of such orders have been issued, and the limit has never been effective. The government and the Bank of England have rejected the idea of a limit, and the Radcliffe Committee endorsed this view almost without discussion; only a few academic economists* still maintain that there is a case for a limit. Characteristically, limitation is opposed on the contradictory ground that it would be ineffective and that it would be so effective as to cause a disastrous bout of deflation.

If there were to be a limit it would probably be best to impose it on the rate of increase of the note issue; a permitted rate of growth of 3 per cent a year would keep the volume of notes roughly in line with the potential growth of output. Notes are, of course, used mainly for wages and small retail transactions and, for these purposes, they have no good substitute. If, therefore, wages rose faster than output and prices went up, the demand for notes would rise faster than the permitted issue, and the reserve of the Bank of

* The limitation of the note issue is discussed by J. Wilson in a paper on 'The Rate of Interest and Monetary Policy' in *Oxford Economic Papers*, October 1957. In some circumstances the limitation of the Treasury bill issue would be an effective substitute for a limitation of the note issue, and suggestions for this were made in evidence to the Radcliffe Committee by Messrs. W. J. C. King and W. Manning Dacy.

England would be depleted. The Bank would then be obliged to raise Bank rate and restrict credit to any extent that might be necessary in order to check the rise in wages and prices. There can be little doubt that this would be an effective remedy, though it would probably be a drastic one; it might involve periods of very high interest rates, and it could, like any effective measure to combat this type of inflation, create unemployment.

The central bank and the government

Closely linked with the question of monetary rules is that of the relationship between the central bank and the government. Many central banks were created by governments and others, like the Bank of England, attained their special position because of privileges granted by the government. They have never been entirely independent and probably never can be. Certainly the enormous growth of government expenditure and government debt during the present century, together with the influence of fiscal policy on demand, economic activity and prices, call for a relationship even closer than before.

It is, however, vital that the central bank should not become the mere servant of the Treasury. The question of ownership is probably not of prime importance here, and a bank that is recognised as a major public agency in its own right may enjoy more effective independence than it could if it were privately owned. It is important, however, that the governor and directors of the central bank should be appointed for long periods, that they should be independent in choosing, training and promoting their officials and that they should keep their methods of recruitment distinct from those of the civil service. In all these ways the bank can be encouraged to cultivate the qualities of mind and outlook appropriate to its special position as guardian of the value of the currency.

Conclusion

The monetary framework of a free society must avoid both inflation and deflation but, so long as government expenditure is maintained at its present level and present attitudes in collective bargaining persist, deflation is unlikely and inflation will be a constant danger. If this threat is to be warded off, price stability needs to be given pride of place among the economic objectives of governments, and they would do well to publicise their determination to stabilise prices as widely as they have done their commitment to maintain full employment. Where fluctuations in prices are linked with cyclical fluctuations in employment there is no conflict between stability of prices and stability of employment. When, however, prices are being pushed upward by pressure on costs, such a conflict may arise, and governments could make it clear that they are prepared, if necessary, to accept an increase in unemployment rather than allow rising costs to be passed on in higher prices. This potential conflict between stability of prices and employment could be resolved, however, if there were a change of attitudes in trade unions and among management so that average wage increases could be kept within bounds set by the average increase in productivity, and prices could fall in industries where progress was at more than the average rate. A more competitive climate which encouraged price cutting would help here, and so would changes in the law with regard to trade unions on the lines suggested by Hayek in another chapter.

Even allowing for these changes, however, some revision is necessary of our notion of what is meant by full employment, though this need not mean a large increase either in unemployment or in unused capacity. Besides helping to preserve price stability a little more reserve capacity would almost certainly make possible a more rapid rate of growth to the eventual benefit of all.

Among the instruments of monetary policy, the power of the central bank over interest rates is still paramount. This power can be made more effective if the government will accept a long-term rate at which it can sell bonds, and so keep down its short-term borrowing. Changes in interest rates can be supplemented by operations on the banks' liquidity ratio, but pressure on them to restrict advances is alien to a free monetary system. For similar reasons restrictions on hire purchase, tempting as they are, should generally be avoided. Some fiscal measures (such as a variable social insurance contribution or sales tax) do not contravene the general principles of a free society and could give valuable support to monetary policy. It is not possible to devise rules of monetary policy that are by any means fully automatic, but discretion has to be combined with discipline. Governments have not shown themselves good at self-discipline in these matters, and there is still a good case for supplementing the external rules provided by the International Monetary Fund with a limit on the rate of increase of the note issue.

FREDERIC BENHAM

Author of numerous books and articles on economics, including several pioneer estimates of national incomes. In 1960 he published (as part-author) *A Short Introduction to the Economy of Latin America*, and in 1961 a short book on *Economic Aid to Underdeveloped Countries*. Best known as the author of *Economics*, an introductory textbook which is still widely used. He has divided his time between university lecturing (mainly at the London School of Economics, where he graduated in 1922) and acting as economic adviser. During the war he was economic adviser to the Comptroller for Development and Welfare in the British West Indies. After a brief return to academic life, he became economic adviser to the Commissioner General for the United Kingdom in South East Asia. Since 1955 he has been Sir Henry Price Research Professor of International Economics. In 1957–8 he was seconded to act as economic adviser to the Chief Minister of Singapore.

VI

Taxation*

F. BENHAM

Progressive taxation

NOBODY advocates that a tax system should be regressive, taking a larger proportion in tax from a lower personal income than from a higher one.† Moreover, it is generally agreed that incomes below a certain level should be exempt from direct taxes such as income tax. The practical issue, therefore, is whether a tax system as a whole and income tax in particular (since it is usually the chief instrument of progressive taxation) should be progressive or proportional on incomes above a certain minimum level.

I leave aside, for the moment, the question whether personal income is the most appropriate criterion or whether some other criterion, such as personal consumption, would be more suitable. I discuss later the method by which incomes from property should be taxed more heavily than incomes from work. It is clear that an income from property is more valuable to its recipient than an earned income of the same size. The former involves no personal exertion and therefore permits complete leisure. Moreover, it can continue indefinitely, whereas the latter may cease owing to the

* This essay was written before the 1961 Budget. The more recent figures on pages 106 and 110 were inserted later.—Ed.

† In fact, a number of tax systems are regressive, not throughout their range but on the poorer families. This is because they include heavy taxes on certain commodities on which the relatively poor spend a larger proportion of their incomes (although a smaller amount) than most taxpayers. Owing to the heavy taxation of tobacco and drink and to taxes on foodstuffs such as tea and sugar, this was the case in Great Britain before the war. It is probably, however, no longer the case in Great Britain today, owing to the post-war rise in the earnings of the lowest-paid workers relatively to the earnings of the better-paid workers, and owing to the greater expenditure of the latter on goods subject to purchase tax.

death, retirement, illness, or unemployment of the earner. Again, property can be used for speculation and can be drawn upon (at the cost of sacrificing the income from the property sold) in case of need.

There is a widespread belief that a tax system should contain a moderate element of progressiveness. A richer man, it is thought, should pay a somewhat larger percentage of his income than a poorer man. For example, if a man with £1,000 a year pays £200 a year in tax, then a man with £10,000 a year should pay rather more than £2,000 a year, possibly £2,500 or £3,000.

In reply to this view, Professor Hayek says (Chapter 20) that experience shows that whenever a mild degree of progressiveness is introduced, it is soon increased until the proportion taken from the higher incomes becomes penally high. Thus, he points out,

> 'it was only in 1910 and 1913 that Great Britain and the United States adopted graduated income taxes rising to the then spectacular figures of 8¼ and 7 per cent respectively. Yet within thirty years these figures had risen to 97½ and 91 per cent' (p. 310).

These very high marginal rates are in accordance with the wishes of the majority of voters, whose motive may be envy (a desire 'to soak the rich'), or a mistaken belief that their own tax burdens will thereby be lightened. In fact, by restricting the flow of investment, especially into innovations and other risky enterprises, by reducing the amount of effort exerted by people of high earning-capacity, and by distorting the price system, heavy progressive taxation tends to keep down the general level of output and earnings. Since it is futile, argues Hayek, to hope that the degree of progressiveness can be kept mild, the best course is to try to keep the tax system as a whole proportional and not progressive.

Many people with a liberal outlook are in favour of reducing the inequality of incomes. They realise that such devices as subsidies on goods and services (for example, on foodstuffs and housing), consumed by the relatively poor, would have harmful effects by distorting the price system. They believe, however, that some reduction in inequality could and should be brought about through 'the mechanism of public finance'.

A partial answer to this view is that under a proportional tax system the effects of inequality can be modified through public expenditure, notably on social services designed to benefit mainly the relatively poor. Another answer is that progressive taxation, unlike proportional taxation, itself distorts the price system. It means that the net return to a man for a given piece of work is lower the higher his total income; it thus discriminates against the man who earns more because he works harder, or because consumers value his services more highly. It also places a premium for those with relatively high incomes on 'doing it yourself'; a man or woman who is heavily taxed must earn several times the amount of the sum paid to a carpenter or a cook in order to cover the payment. Progressive taxation thus not only reduces incentives to work, saving, and investment; it also, by changing the net remuneration for different activities, often diverts people's energies to 'activities where they are less useful than they might be' (p. 317). Hayek considers that this distortion is even more harmful than the weakening of incentives. I return to these and other adverse effects of progressive taxation when I discuss surtax.

Minimum aggregate sacrifice

Hayek's point that once the principle of progressiveness is introduced it is futile to hope that its extent can be kept moderate also applies to 'theoretical' arguments in its favour. 'All arguments in support of progression can be used to justify any degree of progression' (p. 313).

The outstanding illustration of this is the so-called 'principle' of minimum aggregate sacrifice. This 'principle' asserts that in order to raise a given annual sum in taxation, the government should lop off the tops of the higher incomes, reducing them all to the same level. Nobody below that level should pay any taxation and the level should be that at which the sum of the tops lopped off equals the amount required in taxation. This 'principle' was arrived at by reasoning in terms of utility. Utility, sometimes called satisfaction, is what a person is supposed to derive from whatever can be bought with money. It is a feeling, or state of mind, and entirely subjective; therefore it cannot possibly be measured – there are no units in which to measure it. Hence any 'principle' derived from assumptions about utility can be nothing more than an opinion based on introspection or intuition or guesswork.

If, however, we make three questionable assumptions – namely that it is desirable to maximise utility, that anybody would get the same utility as anybody else from an income of any given size, and that the marginal utility of income diminishes (each additional £ a year yielding less additional utility) – we arrive at this 'principle'. Suppose there are only two taxpayers, A with an income of £x + 1 a year, and B with an income of £x a year, and that the government needs £1 a year in taxation. Then the whole £1 should be taken from A and nothing at all from B, for any other arrangement would leave A and B with less utility between them.

Generalising this conclusion, we reach the 'principle' of minimum (or least) aggregate sacrifice. This was advocated by Edgeworth in 1897.* When editing his collected *Papers*, he said that this principle, which he called 'the criterion of good taxation', 'is now very largely accepted'.† In his *Study of Public Finance*, first published in 1928, Pigou says that 'we have one ultimate principle, namely least sacrifice, whose claim is undisputed'.‡

Whether or not complete equality of incomes would be desirable in itself – which is what the 'principle' implies – is a question of opinion. My own view is that even if a completely egalitarian community were possible, it would probably be dull and mediocre, lacking colour, variety, and dynamic impulse. I doubt whether it would provide a setting in which the creative arts would be likely to flourish or the talents of exceptional individuals to be fully developed. However this may be, it seems obvious that the principle of minimum aggregate sacrifice could never be adopted. If every penny of personal income above a certain level were taken in taxation, few incomes above that level would remain in the following years. People with large incomes from property would give some of their property (at least nominally) to their poorer relations or friends, not subject to tax, or would emigrate with it if they could. People with high earning-capacity would also try to emigrate. Incentives to work, save, and invest, in order to obtain incomes above the maximum would be largely destroyed; there would be a drastic fall in the level of national output.

* 'The Pure Theory of Taxation', *Economic Journal*, 1897. This article is reproduced in his *Papers Relating to Political Economy*, Volume II, Section 5 (Macmillan, 1925). Edgeworth says that Professor T. N. Carver was 'the first to propound this doctrine' (of minimum aggregate sacrifice), in his article on 'The Ethical Basis of Distribution' in *Annals of the American Academy of Political Science*, 1895.

† *Papers*, Vol. II, p. 64.

‡ P. 61. Repeated in Third (revised) Edition, 1947, p. 45.

For these reasons the economists who advocated this 'principle' emphatically pointed out that on no account should it be applied. Yet surely this means that they considered other aims, notably the maintenance and increase of national output, more important than their 'principle', which therefore was not really 'ultimate' at all. If economic theory is not to be a guide to economic policy, what use is it?

Hayek seems to share my view, although his comments are more restrained.

> 'There can now be little doubt', [he writes], 'that the use of utility analysis in the theory of taxation was all a regrettable mistake (in which some of the most distinguished economists of the time shared), and that the sooner we can rid ourselves of the confusion it has caused the better' (p. 309).

Hayek's conclusions

Professor Hayek gives a number of impressive arguments against progressive taxation. I have not had the space to repeat them all. What I think he feels most strongly is that it is an intolerable breach of the basic principles of liberty for a majority to impose penal taxation on a minority. I quote his conclusions. What we need is

> 'a rule which, while still leaving open a possibility of a majority's taxing itself to assist a minority, does not sanction a majority's imposing upon a minority whatever burden it regards as right. That a majority, merely because it is a majority, should be entitled to apply to a minority a rule which does not apply to itself is an infringement of a principle much more fundamental than democracy itself, a principle on which the justification of democracy rests' (p. 314).

He thinks that an appropriate rule would be proportional taxation.

> 'It is the great merit of proportional taxation that it provides a rule which is likely to be agreed upon by those who will pay absolutely more and those who will pay absolutely less, and which, once accepted, raises no problem of a separate rule applying only to a minority' (p. 314).

He amplifies this in the last paragraph of his chapter by suggesting that the maximum marginal rate of direct taxation should be the percentage of the total national income which the government takes in taxation. Suppose, for example, that the government takes 25 per cent of the national income in taxation; then 25 per cent would be the standard rate, and also the maximum rate, of income tax. This percentage would be reduced for the lower incomes in proportion to the indirect taxation which they paid; as the higher incomes would pay indirect taxes as well as income tax the net result would be 'a slight over-all progression'.

I am in general agreement both with Hayek's conclusions and with his reasons for them. My chief reservation is that I consider that (in so far as it is possible to separate the two effects) the effect of progressive taxation in reducing incentives is more harmful than its distortion of the price system.

The British tax system

The net receipts from taxation of the British Government for the financial years 1950–51, 1959–60 and 1960–61 may be summarised as follows:

	1950–1	1959–60	1960–61
		£ million	
Income Tax	1,414	2,216	2,433
Surtax	121	182	190
Death Duties	186	226	236
Profits Tax	268	262	263
Stamp Duties	55	98	90
	2,044	2,984	3,212
Motor Vehicle Duties	60	110	126
Taxes on Expenditure	1,628	2,283	2,390
	3,732	5,377	5,728

The 'standard rate' of income tax is at present 7*s.* 9*d.* in the £. But there are various exemptions and allowances, so that the full standard rate applies only to that part of a person's income in excess of at least £500 a year; the corresponding figure is above £1,000 for married men with wholly earned incomes and two or more dependent children. For example, a single person with an income entirely from investment of £500 a year (and no allowances, e.g. for dependent relatives or life assurance premiums) pays £84 and thereafter would pay 7*s*. 9*d*. in the £; if his income were wholly earned the figure corresponding to £500 would be £643; and if his income were wholly earned and he were married without children it would be £772.

Surtax is in effect a part of income tax. It applies (in addition to the standard rate of income tax) on the excess of incomes above at least £2,000 a year. Some of the allowances which apply to income tax (e.g. for a wife, for children, and for part of national insurance contributions) apply also to surtax; but others (e.g. individual allowance, earned income allowance, part of life assurance premiums) do not. The present rates of surtax are 2*s*. in the £ on the last £500 of £2,500 (for a single person with no surtax allowances) and 2*s*. 6*d*. in the £ on the last £500 of £3,000; thereafter the rate rises by 1*s*. in the £ on each additional £1,000 a year up to an income of £6,000 and by 1*s*. in the £ on each additional £2,000 a year up to £12,000 (so that it is 8*s*. 6*d*. in the £ on the top slice of £10,000 to £12,000), and reaches a maximum of 10*s*. in the £ on £15,000 a year and over. Thus, for example, an income of £5,000 a year pays £512 10*s*. in surtax, an income of £8,000 a year pays £1,437 10*s*. in surtax, and an income of £12,000 a year pays £3,037 10*s*. in surtax. (These figures are reduced in so far as allowances can be claimed.) Clearly surtax makes income taxation steeply progressive on the higher incomes.

Death duties (which now consist solely of estate duty) are levied on the 'estate' (assets) of a person who dies. Deductions are allowed for various expenses and for some assets (notably agricultural property) the rates are reduced by 45 per cent. The rates chargeable depend entirely on the value of the estate and not at all on the wealth or incomes of those who inherit. The first £3,000 is exempt. Thereafter the rates are steeply progressive. For example the rate is 15 per cent on an estate of £20,000 to £25,000; 35 per cent on an estate of £50,000 to £60,000; 50 per cent on an estate of £100,000 to £150,000; and 70 per cent on an estate of £500,000 to £750,000. The maximum rate is 80 per cent; it applies to estates of over £1 million. Profits tax is now a flat 12½ per cent on the profits of companies. Stamp duties include a number of duties (for example on cheques) but most of the revenue from them comes from duties on transactions in property, including Stock Exchange securities, the normal rate being 2 per cent *ad valorem*. Motor vehicle duties are taxes on owners of motor vehicles (and include driving licences).

The charges per annum for commercial vehicles vary with the type of vehicle; for private motor-cars there is at present a flat rate of £12 10s. a year.

Taxes on expenditure include taxes on tobacco (£790 million in 1959/60), beer (£219 million), spirits and wines (£170 million), and oil, mainly petrol (£381 million). They include £502 million from purchase tax levied on manufacturers or wholesalers (but paid eventually by consumers) on a wide range of goods (including private motor-cars, on which the rate is now 50 per cent).

Surtax

In my view there is a strong case for the complete abolition of surtax. It is of course the addition of surtax which makes the taxation of incomes so steeply progressive on the higher incomes; the abolition of surtax would leave the taxation of income strictly proportional (above the level, varying with whether income is earned or unearned, the number of dependants, and so forth, at which the standard rate begins to apply).

Over 60 per cent of the total surtax payments are made from earned income. Relatively high incomes are earned by people of outstanding ability in every walk of life. These are the people whose work the community values most highly. Yet surtax heavily weights the scales for them in favour of more leisure. Why should a man already earning, say, £5,000 a year take the trouble to earn an additional £1,000 a year of which the Inland Revenue will take 13*s.* 3*d.* in the £, leaving him with only an additional £337 10*s.*? Why not take long holidays or long weekends instead of exerting himself more, for the benefit of the tax gatherer?

The monetary incentive to 'do it yourself' is no longer so strong as it was when income tax and surtax took 19*s.* 6*d.* in each additional £ from the highest incomes, so that a man might have to earn a further £200 in order to be able to pay £5 to a workman for work done in his home or garden; the corresponding figure to £200 is now little more than £22. But it is still strong, although mitigated by the earned income allowance for married women, in the case of professionally trained wives (including teachers) whose husbands pay substantial surtax. For the incomes of a husband and wife are considered together, as a joint income, for tax purposes. Why should a wife go out to work, however much the community may need her services, when the greater part of what she earns will go in tax? Why not instead do her own housework rather than pay a cook or a charwoman?

It is not possible to measure the extent to which surtax induces people to take more leisure or to do work for themselves instead of earning more. But I think it is significant that nearly four-fifths of all surtax payers have incomes of less than £5,000 a year. Surely quite a number of these, in so far as their incomes are earned, could fairly easily earn still more if they chose.

Great Britain needs more saving, but surtax reduces considerably the net return from saving. Suppose, for example, that a man with an income of £10,000 a year is considering whether or not to save £1,000 for a gross return of £60 a year. Income tax reduces this return to a net £36 7*s.* 6*d.* a year, but surtax reduces it further to a net £10 17*s.* 6*d.* a year. This clearly lessens the inducement to save rather than to consume. It is difficult to estimate how much more private saving would take place in the absence of surtax. In 1959 there were 465,000 persons with incomes before tax of over £2,000 a year, and their total income before tax was £1,815 million. The abolition of surtax would tend to increase both the numbers of persons with incomes of over £2,000 and the size of their incomes; it would leave them with higher incomes after tax; and it would raise the net return on their savings. The resultant increase in private saving would probably be quite substantial.

In several ways surtax tends to reduce the amount of drive and adaptability in the economy, the willingness to make innovations, to try out new products and new methods, to seek out new markets, and in general to take risks. The more successful a risky investment, the larger the percentage of the profit taken in tax, but of course the government gives no compensation for failures. Hence the scales are weighted heavily against innovations and risk-taking.

It is far more difficult than it was a generation or two ago for a man to build up a large enterprise using mainly his own savings as capital. Surtax leaves him with too little income. Hence the individual entrepreneur, the man who backed his own ideas and opened up new types of enterprise, can no longer operate on a large scale unless he has fortuitously acquired enough capital. The men who occupy leading positions in existing companies might conceivably take the place of the self-made entrepreneurs of the past. But here again surtax, with its discrimination against fluctuating incomes, deters them. Instead of accepting mainly an investment income from shares in their company, and putting all their drive into increasing the company's profits, they tend to prefer a fixed salary, with a pension.

Fixed-interest securities in this country yield 6 per cent or more, most ordinary shares only 3 to 4 per cent. One reason for this large difference is that company directors help their shareholders (including themselves) by providing them with untaxed capital gains rather than with considerably higher dividends. Hence too large a proportion of profits is ploughed back into the companies which earn them instead of being distributed in dividends and therefore available for investment in new ventures.* The operations of most companies may be conducted with a high degree of efficiency. But the ideas and enterprise of newcomers are always a valuable dynamic force. It is unfortunate that for various reasons, nearly all connected with surtax, Great Britain derives less benefit from this source than it did before the era of high income taxation.

It is the progressiveness of the income tax system, that is to say it is surtax, which gives rise to most of the problems of taxpayers in seeking legal methods to avoid paying more tax than they need. Many of them employ specialised income tax agents to help them solve these problems. Most arrangements and devices made to reduce the amount of tax liability are the direct consequence of surtax. Most of the effort and ingenuity now employed in discovering and applying these devices could be dispensed with, and most of the headaches and heartaches of taxpayers engaged in continuous wrangles with the Inland Revenue could be avoided, if surtax were abolished.

And why not? The total yield from surtax in 1960–61 was only £190 million, less than 3½ per cent of total tax receipts. The government would not lose all that amount in revenue. Some people of high earning ability would earn more; some people with high incomes would save more; investment would flow to a larger extent into higher-yielding if riskier channels. Higher yields on income tax

* From 1947 to 1958 this harmful effect was accentuated by the misguided practice of discriminating, in the Profits Tax, against profits distributed as dividends. They were taxed, at first, at 25 per cent, whereas undistributed profits were taxed at only 10 per cent. By 1958, when the discrimination was abolished, the tax on distributed profits had risen to 30 per cent, as against only 3 per cent on undistributed profits. See J. Enoch Powell, *Saving in a Free Society*, Hutchinson for I.E.A., pp. 26–31.

(at the standard rate) would offset to a considerable extent the loss of revenue from surtax. And the gain to the economy as a whole would be far larger than any loss to the Exchequer.

I do not suggest replacing surtax by any other tax, for I agree with Hayek that there is much scope for reducing public expenditure. Considerable reductions could be made in expenditure on defence if we gave up trying to become a first-class nuclear power and stopped spending large sums (for little return of any value, up to the present) on the aircraft industry. However, this is partly a technical question, on which I cannot be dogmatic.

There is scope for large reductions in the field of social services. The general principle is that we are now a sufficiently affluent society to strengthen the responsibility of the individual, and provide more flexibility, by leaving arrangements for social security (insurance against various risks) and payments for certain education and health services more to persons as beneficiaries rather than to (largely the same) persons as taxpayers. This would make possible generous and humane treatment under National Assistance to those who genuinely could not afford to provide for themselves and their families. Employers' contributions could remain, as wage-earners would probably be very indignant if they were abolished. But in fact their incidence is almost wholly on the employees, and they are a tax on employment.

Colin Clark has forcibly argued that the wage-earner 'could provide for his own social services, by insuring through trade unions and Friendly Societies, a great deal more advantageously than is at present the case where provision is made by the State.'* In so far as the government continued to run schools, hospitals, and similar institutions, the majority of the people could make substantial contributions to expenditure incurred for their benefit. Nowadays the average manual worker earns nearly £15 a week, and his wife may supplement this by her own earnings. He could surely pay something substantial, directly, towards the education of his children and, say, £5 a week for a hospital bed and the full cost of his drugs, medicines, dentures, spectacles, and so forth.

'Must it be assumed', asks Professor Alan Peacock, 'that because a relatively small proportion of the community may suffer because of personal misfortune or fecklessness, we must have a gigantic

* *Welfare and Taxation*, Catholic Social Guild (1954), p. 60.

pensions scheme for all so that we can avoid operating a means test for a few?'* The new state pension scheme reflects the irresponsible conduct of the government (and of past governments) in saddling the country with a vast liability for future pensions. The aim should be, on the contrary, to make pension contributions and payments a matter for the individual.†

Substantial reductions of public expenditure in these fields and elsewhere (for example, on subsidies to farmers) would make possible the abolition or reduction of other taxes as well as surtax.

Estate duty

I turn to another British tax which I think should be abolished, namely estate duty. Always by far the most important of the death duties, estate duty is now the only tax in this category.

Whatever views one may hold about the extent to which people should be allowed to inherit property, there can be no doubt that estate duty is a bad tax. It is levied only when the owner of property dies. Hence one fortune (technically, 'estate') may be subjected to estate duty several times in the course of a few years, owing to the deaths of successive owners, and almost wiped out, while another may pay nothing at all for, say, fifty years. This is an arbitrary and haphazard method of taxing property.

Further, the rate of tax depends entirely on the size of the estate. The person who inherits pays exactly the same whether he is rich or poor. A man who inherits, for example, five estates of £25,000 each, pays only 15 per cent, that is, £18,750, but if he inherits a single estate of £125,000, he pays 50 per cent, that is £62,500.

Another disadvantage of estate duty is that it can readily be avoided by gifts *inter vivos* made some years before death or by last-minute devices, such as the purchase of real estate in certain countries. The time has come to abolish estate duty and to replace it by a more sensible form of taxation on property.

A tax on personal wealth

The new tax on property which I favour is an annual tax on personal wealth. This would cover not only income-yielding assets but also

* *The Welfare Society*, Unservile State Papers, p. 11.

† See Arthur Seldon, *Pensions for Prosperity*, Hobart Paper 4, Barrie and Rockliff for I.E.A., 1960.

liquid assets such as cash and bank deposits on current account, and assets which yield direct satisfaction to their owner, such as pictures and jewellery. This tax would obviously be less arbitrary, less haphazard, and less subject to avoidance than estate duty.

It would also be preferable to a capital gains tax. If capital gains were taxed, capital losses would be deductible. The yield might therefore be low, at least for considerable periods, as it has been in the United States. Again, if capital gains are taxed only when they are realized, the man who has been fortunate enough to buy securities or real estate which appreciate fairly steadily in value year after year could escape the tax altogether. A capital gains tax of the American type hits mainly the 'in and out' speculator on the Stock Exchange. In this country the 2 per cent stamp duty makes a considerable levy on this type of operator, and he has to pay it whether he gains or loses. A tax on capital gains taxes them only once, when they are realised; but a tax on personal wealth taxes them year after year (at a relatively low rate), provided they are retained.

A tax on personal wealth would raise administrative problems of valuation. The responsibility for declaring each year the market value of all his various assets should be put squarely on the taxpayer, who would be subject to heavy penalties for concealing or fraudulently undervaluing any of his assets. This system works well with income tax; why should it not work for property?

There would be an exemption of, say, the first £10,000. Hence all that most persons would be required to do would be to sign a form declaring that their total assets amounted to less than £10,000 (or, perhaps, £5,000 in order to give the government an opportunity to check the returns of those declaring between £5,000 and £10,000). The number of persons subject to the tax would not be very large. Their holdings of stock exchange securities could be checked against their income tax returns and the valuation would present no difficulty. The values of real estate as assessed by local authorities are mostly out of date and need revising upwards to their current market values. After such revision, these assessments would serve as a check. Banks are already required to report on deposit accounts. Other items, such as valuable pictures and jewellery, would presumably be valued in the same way as they are valued at present for estate duty.

Beyond the substantial exemption limit, further slices of personal wealth would be taxed at low rates. The standard rate would be relatively low, perhaps only 1 per cent. The problem, as with progressive income taxation, would be to keep the standard rate the maximum rate and to prevent it from being raised to penal levels on relatively large personal assets.

Other possible changes

I take this opportunity to give my views, very briefly, on some other possible changes in the British tax system.

The profits tax is a bad tax, for it discriminates against one legal form of business organisation, the company. Companies have to pay profits tax; individual proprietors and partnerships do not. However, the advantages of the company form of organisation are so big for many enterprises, especially those with a large capital, that probably few have been deterred by the profits tax from turning themselves into companies. So long as the profits tax is kept fairly low, and does not discriminate between distributed and undistributed profits, I suppose it can be tolerated for the sake of the revenue it yields.

The stamp duties are heavy, but I think they should be retained. Together with my proposed tax on personal wealth, they would achieve most of the purposes of a capital gains tax without its disadvantages.

Ideally, the present income tax on investment income should be replaced by the personal wealth tax; this would involve making the latter much heavier than I have proposed. I see no reason why one person should be taxed much more lightly than another with assets of the same value because the former chooses to invest his money safely or to buy assets such as pictures which give him direct satisfaction while the latter prefers riskier but higher-yielding investments. The present system of taxing the money yields rather than the assets tends to deter risk-taking. However, I realize that this change would not be accepted by the British Government or electorate.

A major question is whether income should be redefined in order to transform the present income tax into a tax on consumption, or expenditure. The late Professor Irving Fisher urged in numerous writings that income is consumption and that only consumption should be taxed. Withdrawals of capital, gifts and bequests, fortuitous receipts such as winnings from football pools – anything and everything should be counted as income and taxed provided it was spent. But savings should be exempt.

Mr. Nicholas Kaldor, in his book *An Expenditure Tax*, has argued at length in favour of this view. But he wants a personal wealth tax (and a capital gains tax) as well. I agree that assets should be taxed as well as income or expenditure. But while the substitution of an expenditure tax for an income tax of the usual type would remove the differentiation of the latter against saving, taxes on assets would re-introduce it through the back door, by reducing the net return from saving. This cannot be helped. The over-riding principle should be that an income from property is more valuable than an income of the same size from work, and should be taxed more heavily, whether the tax is based on the assets themselves or on the income derived from them.

Mr. Kaldor says that although an expenditure tax is theoretically superior to our present income tax, yet the latter has stood the test of time and on practical and administrative grounds it would be impossible to replace it by the former overnight. I agree. All that he suggests, for the present, is the introduction of an expenditure tax as a partial substitute for surtax. I agree, if surtax cannot be abolished completely.

What about taxes on commodities? At the moment of writing, there is a body of opinion which favours the extension of commodity taxes to a much wider range of commodities, but at relatively low rates. Most of the commodity taxes would be collected from retailers, so that the result would be a sales tax on the lines of the sales taxes in force in many western countries. The purpose would be to make possible reductions of direct taxation by getting more from indirect taxes.

Dr. A. R. Prest, in his thoughtful paper *The Future of Purchase Tax** tends to take this view. He points out that it would be somewhat more complicated to collect purchase tax from perhaps 600,000 retailers than, as at present, from only 62,000 wholesalers. But he urges that the change would stimulate competition and efficiency in retailing. At present 'resale price maintenance rules out price-cutting over a wide range – between a quarter and a half – of consumer

* Hobart Paper 8, Barrie and Rockliff for I.E.A., 1961. Dr. Prest has also written a book, *Public Finance in Theory and Practice* (1960) which contains a stimulating discussion of the advantages and disadvantages of different types of taxes.

spending'. But he hopes, as I do, that resale price maintenance will soon be prohibited.

An advantage of taxing most commodities at a uniform *ad valorem* rate is that this does not interfere with consumers' choice so much as taxing a few commodities at high rates. (It is agreed by nearly everybody, however, that heavy taxation of such commodities as tobacco, with a relatively inelastic demand, should continue.) The disadvantage is that such taxes would fall on everybody, including wage-earners and their families.

I think that our judgment on this question should depend largely on whether or not wage-earners (and others) are made to pay substantial contributions towards the cost of educating their children and of providing themselves and their families with medical attention, hospital accommodation, and so forth. If they are, then I do not think that they should be subjected to taxation on a wide range of commodities in addition to such charges.

In present circumstances I believe that the fewer the commodities subject to tax, whether under import duties or excise duties or purchase tax, the better. Tobacco could bear a considerably higher tax, but not drink, as the revenue would probably increase little and might fall. Private motor vehicles and petrol could be taxed more heavily, although much more than at present should be spent on improving the road system. In general I would like to see as many commodities and services as possible, and certainly all raw materials (such as fuel oil) and means of production, completely free from taxation.

To sum up: I agree with Hayek's criticism of the progressive principle in taxation. It is harmful, I think, mainly because it weakens incentives to effort and investment, innovation and risk-taking. In my view, the main changes required in the British tax system are:

abolition of surtax,
abolition of estate duty,
a tax on personal wealth,
indirect taxes limited to a small number of commodities.

I agree with Hayek that there is wide scope for reductions in public expenditure. This, I think, could largely take the form of reducing the scope of the social services by requiring people to pay for them, thus also encouraging them to make private provision. If this were combined with a generous treatment of those genuinely in need, there could be substantial reductions in the costs of the social services over the next ten or twenty years and therefore in the amount of revenue that it would be necessary to raise by taxation. What is required therefore is not only a reconstruction of the British tax system to strengthen incentives but also a reduction in its level as British society becomes more prosperous.

MICHAEL P. FOGARTY

Born 1916. Educated at Ampleforth College and Christ Church, Oxford. Research assistant at Oxford Institute of Statistics 1940–1, and Nuffield College Social Reconstruction Survey, 1941–4. Official Fellow, Nuffield College, 1944–51. Professor of Industrial Relations, University College of South Wales and Monmouthshire since 1951. Published *Prospects of the Industrial Areas of Great Britain*, 1945, *Town and Country Planning*, 1948, *Christian Democracy in Western Europe, 1820–1953*, 1958, *The Just Wage*, 1961.

VII

Social Welfare

MICHAEL P. FOGARTY

The present state of the debate

FOR the second time in this century the social security systems of Britain and the United States are in a state of revolution. In Britain the first revolution was wound up about 1948; the second is now proceeding.

Towards the end of the nineteenth century there existed in Britain an extensive though incomplete system of voluntary insurance, mainly through friendly societies and trade unions, against sickness and unemployment and for old age pensions; of twelve million workers brought under state health insurance in 1911, five million were previously insured voluntarily. Underlying it was the safety net of a universal system of poor relief.

The first revolution consisted in expanding the state's provision so as to supply besides poor relief benefits available as of right, at the same rate irrespective of earnings, in the main contingencies liable to interrupt earnings or impose exceptional costs;* industrial injuries (1897 and 1906), old age (1908), and sickness, disability, maternity, medical care, and unemployment (1911). These benefits were limited to manual and lower-paid salaried workers. Other benefits, notably dependants' allowances, were added later. At the outset most of these schemes made some attempt to marry state with voluntary administration through insurance companies, friendly societies, and trade unions. The pension scheme was the only one to be administered from the start exclusively by the state.

* *Social Insurance and Allied Services* (the Beveridge Report), Cmd. 6404, 1942, pp. 211 ff.

In the late thirties and early forties these provisions reached the culminating point defined in one of Parkinson's laws: on the edge of obsolescence, they were perfected and consolidated. The lines of consolidation were laid down in the Beveridge Report and carried out in 1945 and 1946. The state took complete responsibility: all schemes were now directly state-operated. The whole population was covered. The lower rates of benefit were raised to the higher, and several major gaps in provisions were filled. The medical benefit under the older schemes was extended into a National Health Service to offer all types of medical service. Children's allowances, hitherto paid only in particular contingencies, were now made available to all families.

But before the cement had set on this massive structure of state security, the second revolution was rocking its foundations. Personal and family insurance has increased, though the extension of state services checked some of its branches (for example insurance for medical care) after 1945. But the dramatic change – it is in this that the second revolution especially consists – is that there has come a rising tide, which during the fifties swelled to a flood, of benefits provided as part of the terms of employment. Today most firms of any size have at least a voluntary contributory sick pay plan, and an increasing number continue pay at full or reduced rates to their manual as well as their white-collar workers. A small but increasing minority promotes plans for additional medical care on the lines of the British United Provident Association, the Hospital Service Plan and the Western Provident Association. The total membership of these schemes exceeded 1 million by 1960, of which perhaps half would be in group – largely occupational – schemes. Pension schemes, which spread rapidly through those public services not yet equipped with them after the First World War and among white-collar staffs in private enterprise during the 1930's, have since the Second World War spread increasingly among manual workers. By 1957 half the adult male work force was earning pension rights outside the state scheme. An increasing number of firms offer supplementary unemployment compensation or severance pay, and a few provide family allowances. Vacation pay, normally equivalent to full rates or earnings, has since the Second World War become a standard term of employment for manual as well as white-collar workers. In 1955 vacation, pension, and sickness contributions by employers, excluding contributions to state schemes, added 16 per cent to the salary bill and 7½ per cent to the wage bill of a sample of seven industries.* The same trend has shown itself in America, with the difference that, whereas in Britain such benefits have been mainly at managements' discretion, in the United States they have to an important extent been established through collective bargaining.

Today in both Britain and America the three levels of provision for contingencies – personal, occupational, and state – flourish alongside and in competition with one another. This has led to vigorous discussion about the proper relationship between them. The debate focuses on three issues: the range of services to be provided, the standard of service to be enforced, and the method by which services are to be financed. It is as a contribution to these debates that Professor Hayek's discussion of social insurance and allied services in Chapter 19 and elsewhere in *The Constitution of Liberty* has to be considered.

Professor Hayek's argument

On the first issue, the range of services to be provided, he has little to say. But on the second, that of the standard and in particular the minimum standard of service, his views are strong and clear-cut. He accepts without question the need for a minimum of public assistance or poor relief. It should be sufficient to ensure food and shelter, but no more, to even the neediest. But beyond that point he sees no objective standard to which social policy could conform. Individuals, no doubt, or particular groups of employers and workers, will have ideas about the amount they wish to set aside for old age or in case of ill-health or unemployment. But these ideas are subjective. A firm line must be drawn between 'a state of affairs in which the community accepts the duty of preventing destitution . . . [and] that in which it assumes the power to determine the just position of everybody' (p. 289). There is no standard above the subsistence line that can be upheld by appealing to 'some non-existent principle of social justice' (p. 302).

This line of thought holds, Hayek argues, for each of the main services that he examines. One cannot say that pensioners need, or

* *Ministry of Labour Gazette*, August 1957. For American data see the special number of the *Industrial and Labour Relations Review* on social insurance, December 1960.

(apart from contractual rights due to their saving) have a right to any particular standard of living above the subsistence minimum. 'In a wealthy society not devastated by inflation it is normal that a large proportion of the retired should be more comfortably off than those still at work' (p. 296). But if they have not earned this position by saving, there is no way of determining objectively what other standard they are to have. One might perhaps say, with the British Labour party, that they should be able to go on living in the same neighbourhood, enjoying the same hobbies, and mixing with the same friends as when they were earning. But what is then to stop the elderly from pitching their demands higher still, claiming greater ease in retirement than they ever enjoyed while working, at least till the youth of the nation, who have force on their side, revolt? (p. 297)

Medical care, in the same way, has no objective standard. One can always spend more on it, especially on the chronic sick, and there is no rule determining the priority that this extra care is to have over other items of expenditure (pp. 298–300). The unemployed worker, for his part, is certainly entitled to any benefit he gets, even above the minimum of subsistence, from his own savings (personal or through a trade union) or through a fund operated on a strict insurance basis, preferably with an element of experience rating, by his firm or industry. But for benefits from other sources there is once again no clear-cut standard to which a minimum unemployment benefit above subsistence level could be related. One might say, Hayek agrees, that since unemployment is often not through a worker's own fault it is unreasonable to throw its whole financial cost above subsistence level on him. But unemployment benefit needs also to be varied in time and amount to promote labour mobility and make it less easy to hold out for excessively high wages. The only clear rule for general, universal unemployment pay, as for other types of benefit, is that it should be confined to subsistence level (pp. 300–302).

On the third issue, that of who is to administer social security and pay for it, Hayek argues forcibly against the three conceptions of state monopoly, finance through redistributive taxation, and commitments that are not covered by invested capital but reach into a later generation.

The state, he agrees, has a role as provider of the last resort. No other agency can guarantee all persons whatsoever against 'the extremes of indigence or starvation due to circumstances beyond their control' (p. 285). It may therefore go further and protect its taxpayers against charges falling on them through the negligence of citizens willing to leave their future to it by compelling all citizens to insure themselves to an extent that will make public assistance unnecessary. This may entail the creation of new and the development of existing means of insurance, and since this is done on the state's initiative the state can properly contribute to the cost of getting them going, though not of administering them thereafter (pp. 285–6). But there must not be a state monopoly even of the minimum compulsory provision, let alone of pensions, unemployment pay, or medical care in general. The case against state monopoly in this field is the same as that against monopoly of any kind in any field.

> 'It is probably true that, at any given moment, a unified organisation designed by the best experts that authority can select will be the most efficient that can be created' (p. 287).

But in the longer run monopoly dries up the springs of innovation. Though performance may remain flawless on the surface, it will not improve or adjust to new needs as it should.

A medical monopoly can guarantee to all 'The bad average standard of service' (p. 299), but progress depends on allowing experiment in service above the average. 'What is . . . possible to provide for all depends on what has already been provided for some' (ibid.): if progress is to continue the pioneering 'some' must be free to seek what they want. Insurance is the creation not of one mind but of millions, and its progress depends on the freedom of its practitioners and customers to experiment. This is as true of social insurance as of any other service. A state monopoly of insurance, by making people less able to help themselves (p. 297), dries up customer initiative. In allied services as well as in insurance, monopoly leads to government by experts, oriented to the state rather than the consumer – the doctor becomes a state servant, and can be exploited by the state, for example for industrial discipline, in ways only too clearly experienced in the Soviet Union (p. 300) – and fundamentally conservative because trained essentially in the working of one particular system and unable to see outside it. It comes naturally to these experts to misuse (in good faith) the compulsorily collected funds to make propaganda glorifying the existing state of affairs.

In the place of state monopoly reliance should be put, Hayek argues, on personal (or family) and occupational insurance, including insurance through trade unions. The state's intervention to ensure a minimum degree of protection should take the form of compulsion on all to insure, but not necessarily or even normally with the state. The dual system whereby the state provides part of everyone's benefits while other means are used to supply the rest should disappear. The state should facilitate other forms of insurance, above all by preventing inflation and maintaining the value of money.

On methods of finance, Hayek notes that commitments reaching into the future, above all in pension schemes which, instead of expecting each generation to provide for its future by capital investment, require it to provide for the old age of the last, have the same defect as a state monopoly. They put a strait-jacket on evolution and limit the next generation's freedom of choice. In addition, as the standard of maintenance expected by old people rises, the commitments impose on successive generations a growing burden from which they will repeatedly try to extricate themselves by inflation (p. 304).

In discussing whether social insurance and allied services are to be financed by beneficiaries or by redistributive taxation, Hayek's argument returns to an earlier issue. The state is justified in financing by compulsory redistribution that part of provision for security that properly belongs to it, namely public assistance, at subsistence rates, for those who can prove extreme need. But above that level there is no objectively just standard of provision which redistribution could be used to achieve. There are only standards determined by personal preference. The right way to make provision for such standards is through the decision of the beneficiary, on his own or in co-operation with others, to allocate part of his income to an insurance or other saving plan. What has happened, Hayek observes, is very different. Social security, though intended in the first place for the relief of poverty (p. 302), has acquired as its chief purpose the redistribution of incomes (p. 288). This has led to difficulty in raising the funds for it (p. 302), to the abandonment of objective standards and the conversion of security (the specific reference is to pensions) into 'a tool of politics, a play ball for vote-catching demagogues' (p. 296), and to the impairment of the income distribution on which the push and pull of a free labour market depends (p. 303).

* * *

The evaluation of Professor Hayek's argument can be summed up into three propositions. When he argues against monopoly and especially state monopoly he is powerful and effective. When he describes the system he prefers and the principles on which it should rest he is sound but incomplete; on some points he is definitely wrong. When he deals with redistribution and long-term commitments his argument is unsatisfying though his conclusions are correct.

State monopoly

Hayek exaggerates the extent of state monopoly in social insurance and allied services in Britain and still more in the United States. In neither country has provision for any of the contingencies he discusses been made a state monopoly in the full and strict sense. The dramatic increase in recent years in non-state provision has for many categories of worker and in a wide range of services reduced state provision to secondary importance. Above all for white-collar workers, but also increasingly for manual workers, the rights to sick pay (in America also to medical care), pension, and severance or unemployment pay earned as part of the terms of employment tend to equal or outweigh those offered by the state. Furthermore, this is not a relic from the past before the advent of state social security. It dates precisely from the time in the last twenty years when state social security as it is known today was reaching or had reached maturity.

But Hayek's argument against state monopoly is nevertheless important and relevant, especially in Britain. In the making of minimum provision, the trend in Britain has been from a partnership between the state and private enterprise towards a complete state monopoly. Though the trend of the state's share in the total of provision for social security has lately been in the opposite direction – this share is smaller today than ten or twelve years ago – this change is by no means universally accepted. The question of creating what in practice though not in principle would be a complete state monopoly is still on the political agenda of at least two services, medical care and pensions below middle management level. British socialists of the strict observance have throughout regarded the element of purchase of service that remains, and indeed is expanding, under the National Health Service as a regrettable survival or sign of reaction, to be done away with at the first opportunity. This objection extends even to co-operative provision; the most remarkable co-operative health plan ever tried in Britain, the Peckham Health Centre, was destroyed by the same Labour government that introduced the National Health Service. The Labour plan for *National Superannuation*, published in 1957, formally left room for private superannuation schemes even for lower-paid workers. But it set terms for contracting out such that the great majority of workers and employers were likely to participate. It also set contributions and benefits at such a level that contributors were likely to have little to spare for supplementary private superannuation and little reason to want it.

Against plans of this kind Professor Hayek's main argument is sound. The swift expansion and multiple experiment in social security and related services in the last few years has been overwhelmingly in the non-state sphere, and there is every reason to think that under a state monopoly it would have taken place on a much smaller scale.

This is not to deny that the state services have been competently run, and with more respect for the personal rights of the citizen than Hayek seems to expect. But competent administration is not the same thing as fresh thinking. What specially bears out his argument is that it is not from the official ranks that the freshest thinking or the most revolutionary experiment has come. The revolution in occupational benefits has been the work of business men and, in America, of trade unionists, not of state servants. It is significant that the British manual workers' unions, which are heavily committed to the idea of state monopoly, have taken almost no initiative in this field. At the academic level readiness to think again about the whole framework of the social services has been found among economists such as Colin Clark, Alan Peacock, Walter Hagenbuch, Peter Wiles or Hayek himself, who have no claim to be specialists in the existing system, rather than among specialists such as Professor R. M. Titmuss and Mr. C. W. Guillebaud who are identified with the social service Establishment.

The service in which expansion has most lagged behind what might have been expected in an increasingly prosperous society is, significantly, National Health, the one that comes closest to a full state monopoly.

Current Expenditures as per cent of Gross National Product

	1949	1950	1959	1960
National Health Service (Britain)		4·19		3·98
Medical care (government and private) (U.S.A.)	4·5		5·5	

Source: D. S. Lees, 'Are We Spending Too Little?', *The Times*, 22nd March, 1961.

In Britain, under state monopoly, the share of the national income used for medical care has stagnated. In the United States, where private or occupational provision predominates, it has steadily grown. It is interesting to speculate on the experiment and new development that might have been possible in the hospital and consultant services since 1948 if a method had been found – as it could be and still can* – of reconciling full insurance coverage for all with free consumer choice of service and the opportunity for hospitals to raise finance directly from the consumer and to plan their spending without the strait-jacket imposed by Ministry budgeting.

British experience underlines Hayek's point (he makes it in relation to the family doctor service) that the danger, not only in a state monopoly but in any state control, is of government not merely by experts but by irrelevant experts. A curious example is the authority exerted by the Inland Revenue over a wide variety of social services. It has assumed authority to determine what is a reasonable level of pension, what form a pension plan should take, whether pension rights may be interchangeable with institutions outside the United Kingdom and to what extent the proceeds of a pension plan may be taken in a lump sum. It sets a limit to the amount of severance pay or supplementary unemployment benefit. It has a similar authority over social policies of other kinds, as for example over the conditions of profit-sharing schemes.† Yet all these are essentially questions of social policy, and should be determined on social grounds: fiscal considerations have at most a marginal part to play.

* Cf. below on the idea of a penal social security tax and of state benefits at rates related to the normal standard of living instead of to subsistence.

† Examples taken from Acton Society Trust, *Redundancy* (1958), and *Wider Shareholding* (1959), and from the Report of the Committee on the *Superannuation of University Teachers*, 1960, especially pars. 16, 40, 85.

The alternative to state monopoly

But what is to take the place of state monopoly? Professor Hayek's picture of the future is up to a point both clear and sound. His stress on the need to avoid inflation has been underlined by the bitter experience of many pensioners in the last twenty years. It has been common for pensioners to find occupational pension rights which should have yielded them half or more of salary at retirement reduced by inflation to a quarter or less. Professions (university teaching, for instance), which in stable conditions would have managed their pension plans wholly for themselves, have been thrown on the mercy of the state and reduced to asking for state supplements and guarantees.

Hayek is also right to forecast the end of the dual system of state and private provision. It is administratively absurd to require persons who can get all the insurance they need from one source (for example an occupational pension scheme) to draw part of it from another, the state, so incurring double administrative costs. There is no need of this duplication to ensure that all carry the necessary minimum of insurance; it is enough to require proof that the necessary insurance, from whatever source, is being carried.

Hayek is right again, in the light of recent history, to assume that (especially with the aid of minimum compulsion) non-state insurance can be extended to give full cover for most if not all major contingencies. It is probably true that to get quick and comprehensive results in social security at the end of the nineteenth and beginning of the twentieth century, with a limited range of techniques and in the face of widespread ignorance and resistance, there had to be a high degree of direct state provision. But today the range of techniques of insurance and of means of educating prospective beneficiaries is far greater than it was then, and the process of educating them has been carried far further.

Even twenty or twenty-five years ago, in the days of the Beveridge Report and the American Social Security Act, it seemed reasonable to doubt whether for the mass of wage-earners non-state benefits would ever be more than a marginal supplement.* But today the time is in sight when even the ordinary wage-earner will have as part of his terms of employment the same high degree of cover as has long been enjoyed by higher salary earners against sickness, old age,

* I.L.R.R., loc. cit., p. 24; cf. also Cmd. 6404.

and (through longer periods of notice as well as one or another form of dismissal pay) in case of changing his job. British experience before the National Health Service – and even under it, in connection with BUPA – reinforces American experience that even without the aid of compulsion both occupational and family insurance for medical care can be extended very rapidly indeed. With the aid of minimum compulsion there need be no difficulty in making it universal.

Yet one would have wished that Hayek could have found more to say about the details of his blueprint for the future, for many of the current practical problems of social security lie in this area. He himself would no doubt say that institutions should be allowed to grow and not be forced, and that in any case a blueprint is out of place in a non-technical discussion. But though the growth of institutions ought not to be forced it can and should often be encouraged. It is also important for the impact of a new view of social security like Hayek's to provide not only criticism of the old order but a vision of the new. On a number of points it would have been useful to hear more.

(1) *The range of services to be provided.* Professor Hayek, though he attempts no general classification of services to be provided, does dismiss somewhat cavalierly family endowment, which has a key part to play in a new view of social security. Family allowances began in Britain as a means of relieving poverty and in France as a way of spreading the impact of the fall in real wages during and after the First World War. Population policy helped in some countries to spread them. But they have continued primarily as a form of insurance or public assistance to meet the costs of one of the most expensive contingencies of life. They may be arranged through the state (including the family man's tax allowances), an employer, or, as with educational endowment policies, through personal insurance. Whatever their form, a policy like Hayek's for increasing people's responsibility for their future is incomplete without them; for only if family endowment is well developed can families with dependent children meet the costs of education, social security, or even housing without strain.*

(2) *The non-state agency most suitable for each service.* The most important substitute for state services is to make provision part of

* M. P. Fogarty, *The Just Wage*, Geoffrey Chapman, 1961, Chs. 7 and 8.

the terms of employment. Personal and family insurance has undoubtedly an important part to play in providing unusual or supplementary benefits. But the essence of social security is setting aside a part of income to provide for contingencies, and the convenient point at which to do this, for the vast majority, is where the wage or salary is received. The check-off of contributions at this point need not interfere with free choice by the contributor. There is for instance no reason why he should not have a free choice between insurance schemes quoted by many independent agencies or (as in many industrial sick pay plans) the chance to contribute additionally for higher benefits. Even where there is a uniform occupational scheme, competition remains. Benefits in one occupation can be compared with those in another, a very powerful factor in raising standards of provision. Quotations from several independent outside sources can be obtained when, for example, investing a pension fund.

But thought needs to be given to the level at which occupational schemes can best be located. These schemes are commonly begun in individual firms. But there is an important range of services, including unemployment pay, pensions, and family allowances, for which on grounds of convenience or risk-spreading the industry may be the most suitable unit. Though for example pensions can be provided through insurance companies by even the smallest concerns, in small-unit industries mobility from job to job is simpler where a scheme covers an industry as a whole.

(3) *The administration of non-state services.* Several problems arise from the multiplicity of agencies under non-state insurance. One is that of preserving pension and other rights on change of employment. Unless they are attached to the insured person rather than to his job or locality there is a danger, though less serious than often supposed,* that mobility in the labour market will be blocked. The American labour movement has gone far to overcome this by collective bargaining: whereas less than 30 per cent of pension plans surveyed in 1952 contained provisions for 'vesting' pensions in the worker, 90 per cent did so in 1959.†

Mismanagement and fraud can occur under both state and private systems, but take a different form and need different treatment, as recent American experience has shown, where service is provided by

* I.L.R.R., p. 30.

† *Labour News from the U.S.*, 23rd September, 1960, supplement.

many separately managed units not subject to continuous public scrutiny.

There can also be – and often is – a paternalism of corporations as well of the state. It is important that corporate provision should take a form, for example through collective bargaining and with a maximum of options for each person, that maximises participation and personal responsibility.*

(4) *The role of the state in a revised structure of social security.* The three previous points are expansions of Professor Hayek's argument rather than criticisms of it. When it comes to the role of the state in a revised security system, it is necessary to be more critical.

In the first place, Professor Hayek understates and in some respects mis-states the grounds on which it is legitimate for either the state or a body at some lower level, such as a firm or a collective bargaining agency, to make provision compulsory. He rightly presents the state's role as educational rather than executive; it is to educate citizens for responsibility, not to take over their responsibilities from them, and accordingly compulsion must be minimised. But it is neither true nor helpful to the acceptance of his case to argue (p. 286) that the ground for such compulsion as remains is chiefly to ensure that the improvident shall not cause expense to others or (p. 285) resort to acts of desperation. Compulsion is justified in the case not only of the improvident, that is of those who could foresee and provide for their own needs but fail to do so, but also of contingencies for which people will wish and might be expected to provide, but whose full implications are not clear to them at the time when provision might best begin to be made. These are commoner than Hayek seems to realise. It is for example unreasonable to expect young people to judge the amount which, looking back from the end of their lives, they will wish to have set aside for their pension as accurately at the age of twenty as they will be able to do at sixty; compulsion by their elders is here certainly justified. And whether in the case of improvidence or of difficulty of foresight, the motive for compulsion is not merely self-protection but solidarity and consideration for the welfare of others.

What provision, secondly, is to be compulsorily enforced?

* Cf. the slashing attack by T. Levitt in the *Harvard Business Review*, September – October 1958.

Professor Hayek answers that, while the state is not in general either to administer or to finance provision for security, it is responsible for ensuring minimum standards and for acting as provider of the last resort, which includes not only public assistance to those with no other means but also the function of reinsurance.

On reinsurance Professor Hayek could with advantage have said more. The state can usefully help non-state insurance by reinsuring or organising the reinsurance of particularly heavy, unpredictable, or long-term risks, for example that of severe unemployment or chronic illness. It has also a role as ultimate guarantor in case of inflation, and this could with advantage be defined. The community is likely to be more careful if its responsibility in case of failure to control the level of demand and prices is set down clearly in advance. Conversely, experience since the Second World War shows that there is likely to be delay and injustice to individuals, especially pensioners, unless the state's obligations in case of inflation are clear and automatic.

But it is on the question of the minimum standard to be enforced that criticism of Professor Hayek's position needs to be sharpest. He argues that the only standard that is objective and universal enough to be enforced is subsistence. This is ordinarily understood, not in its literal meaning of bread and water, but as something a little below what is currently established as the standard of living of an unskilled labourer. It is thus a conventional rather than an absolute standard. Professor Hayek agrees (pp. 285–6) that some such interpretation of it is both inevitable and acceptable. It is true that this is one standard below which it is agreed that those to whom it is appropriate – the members of a particular economy or labour market, since this is the unit for which a conventional subsistence standard is set up – ought not to be allowed to fall. But there is also another standard, likewise varying from one economic group to another, but conventionally identifiable in each group, which it has become increasingly apparent that people will wish to provide for themselves in illness or old age, and whose absence they feel as a deprivation. It is correctly described by the Labour Party* as the standard which will allow continuity in respects such as the district one lives in and the circles in which one has friends, and by a recent writer in the *International Labour Review* as the standard that allows

* *National Superannuation*, 1957, p. 30.

one to maintain the status acquired through work.* In a field like that of the Health Service, it might be defined as the standard that lets one obtain an ordinary or average standard of medical care without sacrificing the standard of living acquired by work. It is this standard, not subsistence, that is relevant to the provision to be made for people at economic levels above that of an unskilled labourer, and if there is to be compulsion to insure it is this rather than subsistence that it is reasonable to enforce. A maintenance-of-status standard, like a subsistence standard, is likely because it is conventional to be somewhat arbitrary, and to be found within a certain range of incomes rather than at a precise point. Since the state is concerned only with minimum standards of security, its business will be not to enforce what is for each person the actually preferred standard of security, whether subsistence or maintenance-of-status, but to mark the lower end of the bracket within which preferred standards lie.

How is the state to enforce a minimum standard, however that may be defined? The simplest and most effective method would seem to be that of a social security tax, from which those who show proof of non-state insurance can be exempted in whole or in part. The tax and the benefits to which it entitles the taxpayer can be set at a level that on the one hand renders it highly unprofitable for the taxpayer to rely on state security instead of seeking other means of insurance, and on the other enables the state to recover from the negligent not only the cost of services supplied to them but also a contribution to the general administrative cost of checking the insurance of those who provide for themselves in other ways. It is reasonable that the foolish should in this way pay not only for their own supervision but also for the supervision that their foolishness makes it necessary to impose on the wise.

A social security tax of this kind is the largest part of the answer to a question about which Professor Hayek appears somewhat pessimistic, that of the winding up of the state's detailed involvement in the running of social security and allied services. The credit side of this involvement is that it has made possible the establishment of general minimum standards of income insurance and medical care. The debit side has been the discouragement of initiative by families or through collective bargaining through the monopolisation of

* E. Liefmann-Keil, in *International Labour Review*, May 1959, p. 401.

wide sectors of social insurance by the state. The problem is to get rid of the debit while keeping the credit, and a penal social security tax shows the way. Those who choose to pay the tax keep their title to adequate minimum standards of security, but at heavy cost. The pressure is on them all the time to seek other ways of meeting their needs, and, as they shift one after another of their provisions to non-state channels, their liability to the tax can be progressively reduced. The successive reduction of tax will help to bring home to beneficiaries that it is the citizen himself who pays for state benefits, and that the extra amount he pays to provide himself with, for example, an occupational pension is a replacement of what he might otherwise have paid to the state and not an addition to it.

The finance of social security

Professor Hayek's discussion of the finance of social security is somewhat unsatisfactory, not so much for its conclusions as for its line of argument.

First, he over-estimates the extent to which social security does in fact serve as an agency of redistribution. In so far as state social services are financed by employee contributions, their cost falls on employees themselves. In so far as they are financed by employer contributions they form part of the cost of employing labour, and it is reasonable to suppose that their general cost – apart from any special or exceptional charge falling on a particular firm – will fall mainly on employees through higher prices or lower direct wages.* The cost of tax-financed social services in Britain falls mainly on the same classes that benefit from them. The working class, in particular, pays for most of its own social services.† Such true redistribution through taxation as does occur arises mainly from three causes: subsidising those altogether without resources, making good the loss caused to individuals by the failure to control inflation, and bringing into social security schemes from the start those who, because of the absence of such schemes in the past, have not paid actuarially adequate premiums. The first of these reasons is acceptable to

* Cmd. 6404, par. 276; cf. on French experience J. T. Dunlop (ed.), *The Theory of Wage Determination*, p. 252; for a contrasting and critical view, see R. A. Lester in I.L.R.R., loc. cit., p. 57.

† Clark, *Welfare and Taxation*, 1954, though his case is over-stated. On his figures the working class must have received a subsidy, if not in respect of social services, then certainly in respect of other public services.

Professor Hayek, and the second he regards as at least tolerable once inflation has taken place. The third, though he rejects it, would seem to fit into his category of expenses reasonably necessary for the launching of new social security schemes.

This over-estimation of the extent of redistribution leads Professor Hayek to give undue prominence to the question of means tests. He is of course right to say that anyone who asks his fellow-citizens for gratuitous aid, justified purely by need and not by any contract or contribution on his part, and calls on the state to compel them to give it to him, must expect to have the genuineness of his need tested. But the number of such cases is actually much smaller than Professor Hayek thinks. The normal case is that of a man who pays taxes and contributions and in return receives benefits with only that kind of redistribution which occurs in any insurance scheme, plus that which arises from the role of the state as ultimate guarantor against inflation or as initiator of insurance schemes. In practice gratuitous aid is limited to two cases. One is that of the person who is no longer a family dependent but has had no opportunity to acquire rights through his, or more often her, contribution to insurance or taxation. This case might be better thought of as arising through one of those extraordinary risks for which the state acts as ultimate insurer. Benefits under it would then be treated as justified by the contributions of the beneficiary's family if not by his own, and a means test would be out of place. The other case is that of the malingerer. Here of course a strict and indeed penal means test is justified.

The real case against redistribution, except as a measure of last resort, lies in two arguments on which Professor Hayek lays less stress. First, even nominal redistribution, such as occurs in the British tax-financed social services, breaks the clear link between effort and reward and removes the stress on personal responsibility whose importance *The Constitution of Liberty* rightly underlines. Still more, of course, does effective redistribution. Secondly, to treat redistribution – in other words, an assault by one class on the income of another – as an essential ingredient in social security is to raise a serious and unnecessary opposition to its development. In countries like Britain where redistribution has been treated as at least in principle one of social security's essential ingredients,* this has certainly been a factor in the difficulty of raising funds for it in

* Cf. Cmd. 6404, par. 273.

recent years. It has also led to unnecessary argument over the height of social security standards.

There is also some lack of balance, though not enough to upset the argument, in Professor Hayek's discussion of the danger of commitments by one generation against the next, particularly in connection with pensions. Continuing corporate bodies such as trade unions,* firms, and the state always have used and still do use the technique of assessment or 'pay as you go', that is of financing pensions in whole or in part, not with an invested fund but through a levy on their members when the pensions became due. This technique, Professor Hayek rightly points out, can easily lead to a rapidly rising burden of pensions. This is particularly true when a pension plan is starting or when the age-composition of the population is changing and the proportion of the elderly is growing. Even in a continuing scheme and with a balanced population, the levy required to pay for pensions on this basis may easily be twice as high – or more – as the premium needed under a funded scheme, for under funding the interest on investments may well cover half the benefits paid. It is perfectly correct to say that in these conditions the younger generation may feel pensions as a heavy burden and be faced with a choice between denying their obligation to the old and incurring a heavy double cost – of current pensions to the old plus contributions to a fund for their own pensions in future – if they wish to switch to another system. † This is what Professor Hayek means when he talks of putting the next generation into a strait-jacket. The use of the assessment system for pensions is a further reason why, even with the aid of repeated political agitation, the British state social security system has obtained in recent years barely enough funds to keep pensions and sick pay in the same low relation to earnings as before the First World War.

But one could wish that the argument had been balanced differently. Though the assessment system is imperfect and sometimes dangerous – it is today illegal for insurance companies – it can be and is made to work after a fashion, especially in a state social security system backed by the power of taxation. It even has certain advantages, for in a rapidly changing modern economy, subject to

* This point is fully considered by S. and B. Webb, *Industrial Democracy*, Longmans, 1902, pp. 152 ff.

† Cf. *Superannuation for University Teachers*, pars. 16–22.

the risks of war and political crisis, a guarantee from the state to use its taxing power to underpin pensions may actually be safer than the attempt to build up an investment fund, or at least is a useful supplement to it.* It would therefore have been useful to reinforce the attack on assessmentism with a more positive statement of the case for funded pensions.

This case rests, apart from the defects of the assessment system, particularly on two points. One is that there is in the world today, and is likely to be for as far ahead as it is useful to plan, an acute shortage of capital. A policy that encourages accumulation is therefore always to be preferred to one that does not. The other is that there is a strong case (though this is not the place to argue it) for spreading capital ownership widely, roughly perhaps in proportion to income. For achieving this end, funded pensions are the most powerful device ever invented.†

Conclusion

In the last few years there have been two main streams of thought in Britain about social insurance and allied services, one justified by socialism and the other by liberalism. The liberal approach parallels Hayek's, and has had an increasing impact even outside the Liberal Party. In the twenty years since the Beveridge Report, social and economic development has enforced a revolution in social and economic thinking. In 1942 the vision was of an all-embracing state structure of social services. In the 1960s the vision is of increasingly independent individuals who make use of a variety of means – state, occupational, personal – for providing against the common contingencies of life. Some economists have been contemplating a gradual winding-up of state services, inspired by the view that, in Professor Peacock's words:‡ 'The true object of the Welfare State . . . is to teach people how to do without it.' It would seem that economists and other social scientists in the 1960s will be increasingly concerned, not with the welfare state as we have come to think of it, but with the institutional structures that could be devised to take its place.

* Cf. J. Douglas Brown in I.L.R.R., loc. cit., p. 110.
† Fogarty, op. cit., ch. 11.
‡ *The Welfare Society*, Unservile State Papers, Liberal Party publication, 1961.

THE RT. HON. SIR HENRY SLESSER, P.C., Q.C.

Educated at Oundle and St. Paul's Schools and University of London. Called to the Bar in 1906. Bencher of Inner Temple, 1924. K.C., 1924. Labour M.P. for South-East Leeds, 1924–9. Solicitor-General in the 1924 Labour Government. A Lord Justice of Appeal, 1929–40. Published *Trade Union Law* (3rd Edition), 1928, *Law* (*Heritage Series*), 1936, *Judgment Reserved*, 1941, *The Judicial Office*, 1943, *Order and Disorder*, 1945, *The Administration of the Law*, 1948. Lives in Devon, where he is an alderman of the County Council and Chairman of the Dartmoor National Park Committee.

VIII

Trade Unions and the Labour Market

Part 1: The Legal Status of Trade Unions

SIR HENRY SLESSER

WRITING on 'Labour Unions and Employment' (Chapter 18), Professor Hayek asserts that:

> 'Public policy concerning labour unions has, in little more than a century, moved from one extreme to the other. From a state in which little the unions could do was legal if they were not prohibited altogether, we have now reached a state where they have become uniquely privileged institutions to which the general rules of law do not apply' (p. 267).

The main powers which these privileged institutions wield, says Hayek, are those of coercing or intimidating fellow-members of trade unions and non-members by mass picketing and other means to withhold their labour in the event of strikes (p. 274), of restricting the numbers of employees in particular trades by closed or union shops (p. 275), and of forcing other workers to fall in with union policies by secondary strikes or boycotts (p. 275).

How far this is justified – Hayek is not particularly concerned with English law as such – raises sociological rather than legal questions, but confining myself to juristic matters I must admit that trade union law is in a very anomalous condition. The Royal Commissions of 1867, 1874 and 1906, with consequent legislation have, if anything, confused the law still further.

It must be said that in every case they were dealing with a very controversial situation. At common law trade unions, which had arisen in the eighteenth century to raise wages by withholding labour, were certainly in whole or in part combinations in restraint of trade; but, apart from their legal status under the Combination Acts of

1800 (which were repealed in 1824 and 1825), the better opinion is that they were never criminal conspiracies at common law.

Origins of trade union laws

The authorities seemed to differ how far a trade union was unlawful before the Trade Union Act of 1871. In 1855* Lord Campbell thought it was lawful, but Crompton, J., disagreed. In 1866 Cockburn, C. J.† favoured such combination as lawful, and quoted Lord Campbell as having expressed a strong opinion in favour of the right of labour to combine to raise wages, but in 1861,‡ as in 1855, Crompton, J. had taken the opposite view.

From early times, on the other hand, combinations in restraint of trade were made illegal conspiracies by *statute*, partly because the state for a very long time itself regulated the conditions of labour, partly because of an early belief, outside the strict domain of state control, in freedom of trade, and partly from a general aversion, not confined to English law, to combinations within the state which might possibly be hostile to it. Among early statutes dealing with criminal combinations are to be noted three Acts of Edward I and the Statutes of Labourers, 1349 and 1350 (applied as late as 1818 to a combination to raise wages among cotton spinners), both of which themselves fixed wages and made the evasion of their provisions criminal. Other similar statutes were passed in the fourteenth, fifteenth and sixteenth centuries; for example, one forbade 'the annual congregations and confederacies made by masons in their general chapters assembled to violate the Statutes of Labourers'.

In Scotland, however, according to Burnett, 'a combination to alter the price of labour was held to be indictable *at common law*' and similar legislation in 1411 preventing combination dealt specifically with 'the fees of craftsmen, and the price of their work'. Other Acts with similar intent were those of 1413 and 1426. An Act of 1547 dealt with 'the price of craftsmen's work'. All these Acts forbade combinations.

By later legislation combination among silk-workers was forbidden in England in 1662, and tailors' wages were regulated and agreements to raise them made illegal in 1720. In 1725 'An Act to prevent unlawful combinations of workmen employed in the woollen manufactures, and for the better payment of their wages' was passed. This

* *Hilton* v. *Eckersley*. † *Wood* v. *Bowron*. ‡ *Walsby* v. *Anley*.

was followed in 1730 in Ireland by 'An Act to prevent unlawful combinations of workmen in all trades'. An Act of 1748 applied to the hat trade, followed by a further Act of 1755 which, remedially, provided for the almost obsolete fixing of piecework rates by the justices. In the reign of George III, before the turn of the century, some fifteen or sixteen other Combination Acts were passed making unlawful combines in particular trades.

In 1799 all combinations of workmen to regulate the conditions of their work were declared illegal, and in 1800 the Combination Act of 1799 was amended and a new general consolidating Act 'to prevent unlawful combinations of workmen' became law. This Act only differed from that of 1799 in providing machinery for arbitration. By this Combination Act of 1800 *every* combination for obtaining an advance in wages, altering the hours of work, or decreasing the amount of work or preventing any person employing whomsoever he might think fit to employ, or for preventing workmen hiring themselves, or attempting to induce workmen to leave their work, was declared illegal; so also was attending any meeting called to advance any of these objects.

Before this general legislation, apart from specific prohibition of strikes, acts had been passed with the express purpose of preventing incipient trade unionism – as those of 1774, which forbade combinations among weavers; 1777 (silk-weavers); and 1795 (hat trade). Then, in 1824 the Combination Laws Repeal Act removed all criminal liability of combinations incurred by advancing or fixing the rate of wages or altering the hours or quality of work imposed either by statute or common law. In 1825 an amending and qualifying Act specifically created new offences of 'molestation, intimidation, threats and obstruction', which applied to individuals as well as to combinations, to force or prevent a person accepting or giving employment or joining any association. An Act of 1817, which provides that a society employing delegates or committees is an unlawful combination, is still unrepealed, as is also the Act of 1799, which forbids combinations and unlawful oaths, but there are no reported cases on unlawful oaths later than 1834.

After 1825, therefore, in general, a combination in restraint of trade for a *bona fide* trade purpose ceased to be a criminal offence so far as statute law was concerned. At common law, as I have said, it is now the better opinion that such a combination was never criminal, though the contrary opinion has in the past been held, but not always. Thus, Hawkins's *Pleas of the Crown* (1717) said that:

> 'all confederacies whatsoever wrongfully to prejudice a third person are highly criminal at common law, as when divers persons confederate together by indirect means to impoverish a third person,'

but such an opinion was dissented from by Holt, C. J. in 1704,* who held that the criminal element in cases in 1662† and 1664,‡ on which Hawkins based his *dicta*, arose in respect of conspiracies against the state, and that, therefore, they were no authority in respect of combinations which had no such anti-governmental objects or effect. These decisions are still of importance in considering the law regarding general strikes.

According to Mr. Justice Wright,§ a suggestion of a general doctrine that a combination may be criminal, although what it proposes would not be criminal apart from combination, begins to appear in the arguments of counsel towards the close of the seventeenth century.|| One of the few early reported cases in which a conviction for conspiracy at common law to raise wages was sustained was in 1721,¶ which is of doubtful authority, and on this case was founded the *dictum* of Grose, J., in 1798,** that:

> 'in conspiracy to raise wages, if several meet for the same purpose, it is illegal and the parties may be indicted for conspiracy.'

Thus, even after the passing of the Combination Laws Repeal Acts of 1824 and 1825, opinion became prevalent among some of the judges that conspiracies in restraint of trade were criminal offences at common law, and a number of cases were decided in accordance with that doctrine. But it may fairly be said that before 1800 there is no suggestion as to criminality in combinations of workmen at common law in the textbooks (Wright). In Burn's *Justice* (1810), the only offences stated are statutory ones.

Finally, a judgment in 1872†† added to the confusion. Owing to a strike of gas-stokers London was deprived of light, and the men were indicted for a conspiracy to coerce or molest their employers in

* *R.* v. *Daniell.* † *Kimberty.* ‡ *Sterling.*

§ *Law of Criminal Conspiracies and Agreements*, 1873, p. 11.

|| *R.* v. *Sterling* (1665), *Thorpe's Case* (1696), *Best's Case* (1705), and *Vertue* v. *Lord Clive* (1769).

¶ *R.* v. *Journeymen Tailors of Cambridge.*

** *Rex* v. *Mawbey.* †† *R.* v. *Bunn.*

carrying on their business. It was held by Lord Esher that there was an indictable conspiracy, because at *common law* it was an indictable conspiracy to force the company to carry on their business contrary to their own will by improper threats or molestation. Hence the great public inconvenience from such a strike, in his view, might be an improper molestation, and a threat of a simultaneous breach of contract might amount to a conspiracy to prevent the employer from carrying on his business.

In the words of Mr. Justice Stephen:

> 'This case substantially decided, as far as its authority went, that, although a strike could no longer be punished as a conspiracy in restraint of trade, it might, under circumstances, be of such a nature as to amount to a conspiracy at common law to molest, injure, or impoverish an individual, or to prevent him from carrying on his business.'

In consequence of this decision, a Royal Commission was appointed in 1874, and as a result the Conspiracy and Protection of Property Act, 1875 was passed which nullified that decision. Together with the earlier Act of 1871 and the Trade Disputes Act of 1906, it now constitutes the principal statutory law affecting a trade union in its criminal aspects.

The growth and use of picketing

Professor Hayek is concerned with the possible use of 'the picket line as an instrument of intimidation' (p. 274) and, so far as the law of England is concerned, two Acts, those of 1875 and 1906, have endeavoured to lay down the law on this matter.

By the former Act it was provided that any person who:

(1) 'uses violence to or intimidates such other person or his wife or children, or injures his property; or,
(2) 'persistently follows such other person about from place to place; or,
(3) 'hides any tools, clothes, or other property owned or used by such other person, or deprives him of or hinders him in the use thereof; or,
(4) 'watches or besets the house or other place where such other person resides, or works, or carries on business, or happens to be, or the approach to such house or place; or,
(5) 'follows such other person with two or more other persons in a disorderly manner in or through any street or road,

shall, on conviction thereof by a Court of summary jurisdiction, or on indictment as hereinafter mentioned, be liable either to pay a penalty not exceeding twenty pounds, or to be imprisoned for a term not exceeding three months, with or without hard labour.'

To this must be added the 'peaceful picketing' section of the Trade Disputes Act 1906, to the effect that:

'It shall be lawful for one or more persons acting on their own behalf or on behalf of a trade union or of an individual employer or firm in contemplation or furtherance of a trade dispute, to attend at or near a house or place where a person resides or works or carries on business or happens to be, if they so attend merely for the purpose of peacefully obtaining or communicating information or of peacefully persuading any person to work or abstain from working.'

The attempt made by the Trade Disputes Act 1927 to redefine these provisions has no legal validity today, as that Act, save in Northern Ireland, has been repealed; but its provisions dealing with picketing might have gone some way to satisfy Hayek. Thus 'Intimidation' therein received a new definition to include as illegal:

'to cause in the mind of a person a reasonable apprehension of injury to him or to any member of his family or to any of his dependants or of violence or damage to any person or property, and the expression "injury" includes injury to a person in respect of his business, occupation, employment or other source of income and includes any actionable wrong.'

Before the Trade Disputes Act of 1906, it had, however, been judicially declared that:

'to tell an employer that his shop would be picketed in threatening language did not amount to statutory intimidation, nor to tell an employer how many apprentices he should employ.'

This in effect was enacted by the 1906 Act and is still law. How far the 1927 Act would have enlarged the ambit of 'intimidation' it is not easy to say, as no cases were decided under it before it was repealed. The intention was certainly to extend the possibility that 'apprehension of injury', personal or proprietory, might amount to intimidation.

Perhaps the more drastic attempted alteration to the existing law on picketing was sought to be made under the 1927 Act by an enlargement of the 1906 definition relating to 'Watching and Besetting'. The 1927 Act provided

> 'that notwithstanding anything in any Act it shall not be lawful for one or more persons, for the purpose of inducing any person to work or to abstain from working, to watch or beset a house or place where a person resides or the approach to such a house or place, and any person who acts in contravention of this subsection shall be liable on summary conviction to a fine not exceeding twenty pounds or to imprisonment for a term not exceeding three months.'

There are few cases since 1906 dealing with alleged intimidation; those which have arisen have been dealt with, mostly, as matters of fact.

There is, however, a cognate matter, to which Professor Hayek makes little reference: the possible coercion of persons other than workmen by commercial or professional trade unions. Generally speaking (apart from the restrictive practices and monopolies legislation), it has now been decided in many leading cases in the House of Lords that to pursue supposed trade interests, individually or in association, is justified even though it results in injury to another, consequential and not primarily intended.* The *Thorne* case decided finally that to place an offending trader on a black list or warn others not to deal with him was not in itself a civil or a criminal wrong – thus resolving differences which had arisen between the Court of Appeal and the Court of Criminal Appeal on this issue.

Thus, like picketing, 'black lists' and similar methods of persuasion or coercion are not normally unlawful unless they contain defamatory matter. It will be remembered that the coercion employed by such commercial trade unions are not, as a rule, physical in their nature but rather economic or psychological. Hence direct problems of picketing and 'besetting' do not arise, but the problem what constitutes 'intimidation' is common to all trade unions of whatever type.

The 1871 Act

The *civil* situation is different, and as late as 1867 it was decided that a union whose member had defrauded it could not sue him by reason of the doctrine of restraint of trade. Hence the Act of 1871 which declared that a trade union, by reason only of its being in restraint of trade, could nevertheless generally enforce its contract.

* *Mogul* case (1892), *Sorrel* v. *Smith* (1925) and *Thorne* (1930).

So also any earlier suggestion that for such reason it might be deemed criminal so as to make a member liable to prosecution was declared to be invalid.

Had the matter ended there it might be said that the position had been effectually clarified. But the Act went on to say that no court could entertain proceedings to enforce directly or recover damages for the breach of agreements between members of a union as to how they might transact business, employ or be employed. Agreements under the rules to provide benefits to members or pay fines or subscriptions were similarly excluded. If the union, despite its having certain rules in restraint of trade, were held to be substantially lawful at common law, no recourse to the 1871 Act was necessary and the exclusion of inter-union agreements did not apply. Consequently, and paradoxically, it emerged from a mass of litigation that the union in seeking to resist a claim for benefit by a member would argue its own illegality while the member would seek to draw from its rules a decision of the union's common law innocence!

The view that combinations to perform acts not in themselves torts* might become tortious when done in combination by unlawful means became prevalent in Victorian times, and it was extended to cover the case of combinations to raise wages, as appears in the not easily reconcilable cases in 1898† and 1901‡ in the House of Lords.

Thus while it is true that occasional *dicta* are to be found to the effect that combinations to better the conditions of labour are unlawful at common law, the Courts have never accepted the law thus laid down, and eminent judges have expressed views to the contrary. Throughout the seventeenth and eighteenth centuries no Court treated combinations to better the conditions of labour as contrary to common law, and none of the series of legislative enactments resisting attempts of workmen to better the conditions of labour purported to declare or rest upon the common law. If we except an *obiter dictum* by Grose, J., in 1798, which was not intended to refer to the common law, but to the effect of statutes then in force, there were no judicial *dicta* in support of the suggested proposition until after the legislature swept away all those statutes by the Combination Act of 1825.

The matter came to a head when, in 1901, the House of Lords in

* For example, preventing contracts being made, as distinguished from the wrongful procurement of their breach.

† *Allen* v. *Flood*. ‡ *Quinn* v. *Leathem*.

the Taff Vale Case dealt with the interference of a trade union with a railway company both by procuring breaches of contract by the employees and preventing new contracts being entered into. No discrimination appears to have been made between the first act, clearly unlawful, and the latter, doubtfully so. It held the union and its officials financially responsible for the damage undoubtedly suffered. The responsibility was placed upon the union for the alleged wrongful acts of its servants in the course of their duty, a decision almost indisputable in law.

The 1906 Act

No one could argue, save as regard the *prevention* of new contracts, that the decision of the House of Lords was not legally correct. But the economic and social consequences of the decision were such that, after the consideration of a Royal Commission in 1906, the government presented to Parliament a Bill which provided that where a committee had been appointed to conduct a trade dispute, an action in which it sought to charge the funds of the union with damages in respect of a wrongful act *in contemplation or furtherance of a trade dispute* should not lie unless the act was committed by the union committee or someone authorised by them.

This provision, drafted by the Attorney-General, and comparatively innocuous, was however amended into something very different and far more opposed to common law principles. The Trade Disputes Act 1906 (Section 2), as finally passed, exempted trade unions of all types from *all* actions in tort. It was not confined to any matter concerning trade disputes but extended to a protection from suits for civil wrongs, libel, negligence or the like. An obscure addition appears to limit the protection afforded to trustees in certain proprietory matters.

But, however necessary a protection for the union (including among its funds assets for sick and unemployment and funeral benefits) which under the Taff Vale Case would all have been liable for damages, the same argument can scarcely be applied to Section 3. It dealt with individual as distinct from union liability and provides that:

> 'an act done by a person in contemplation or furtherance of a trade dispute is not actionable on the ground only that it induces some other person to break a contract of employment or is an interference with the trade, business, or employment of some other

person, or with the right of some other person to dispose of his capital or labour as he will.'

We may note in passing that it was decided in the House of Lords in 1909* that this protection attaches to 'sympathetic' strikes (which Professor Hayek expressly condemns) and, presumably, to lock-outs and similar commercial interferences.

This drastic exclusion from normal liability for the procurement of breaches of contract in the circumstances mentioned is, perhaps, unique in English legislation. Whatever may be the legal niceties arising in the case of combinations for trade or labour protection and those arising normally from the exigencies of competition, there is no doubt as to the liability for procuring breaches of contract between others. The liability of one person for interference with another's right to dispose of his labour or capital without the use of specifically illegal means is more uncertain, but if we confine our consideration to the wrong of procurement of breach of contract, there is no doubt that Section 3 of the Trade Disputes Act of 1906 does, in popular language, place trade unions 'above the law'.†

The status of a trade union

As to the nature of trade unions as such, the definition of a trade union before the passing of the 1871 Act is obscure. Certain observations however may safely be made. First, a trade union never had and has not now corporate status – it is a combination of persons (whether of workmen, capitalists, or professionals) normally bound to one another by rules and trusts, sanctioned by fines and penalties and financed by subscriptions, whether of a permanent or temporary nature. In this it resembles other unincorporated bodies such as friendly societies and clubs, both of which generally have their property held by trustees according to their respective constitutions and objects. In their earlier days, we may note, some trade unions bound their members together by oaths, a practice which, as has been said, was forbidden by the Unlawful Societies Act of 1799, followed in 1817 by an Act forbidding seditious meetings, which were being construed in certain cases to cover what would now be considered to be normal trade union activities.

* Conway's case.

† The analogy of the Gaming Acts by Darling, J. on addressing a jury in *Dallimore* v. *Williams* (1912) was expressly disapproved in the Court of Appeal.

Although trade unions have for their essential development those restraints on the liberty of their members, whether workmen or capitalists, to dispose of their labour or commerce as they wish – purposes said in general to be as the law puts it, in 'restraint of trade',* the earliest workers' combinations appear to have been directed rather to the enforcement of the Elizabethan Statute of Apprentices. This and similar Acts empowered the justices to fix wages, but by the eighteenth century the procedure had become quite ineffective. Then it was that trades clubs and trade unions, such as the Tailors and Weavers Unions in 1720, came into being overtly to act in restraint of trade. And they have continued their operations, the employers and manufacturers following them, until the present time.

The Osborne judgment

The law, having once proclaimed by statute their legality, while still holding other contracts generally in restraint of trade to be unenforceable, was content to leave trade unions in their anomalous condition until, in 1910, the House of Lords was compelled to examine their legal status in a manner which had never been attempted before. This obligation arose from the fact that in 1908 one Osborne, a member of a trade union, the Amalgamated Society of Railway Servants, had invoked the law to prevent the Society from spending its money upon political objects. Had the union been a corporation, constituted by charter or under statute, the House and the lower courts would have sought to find the limits of its powers in the terms of the charter or articles of association. It was, however, common ground that the trade union, though registered under the Trade Union Act 1871, had no corporate *persona* beyond its power to sue or be sued in its registered name. Recourse, therefore, was made to the principle that bodies constituted by statute, even though not corporations, could not act beyond the powers directly or inferentially conferred upon them, and that this was the case with a trade union. It was said that the definition in the 1871 Act, though wide

* Professor Hayek contends that trade unions pursue sectional interests: 'Few liberal sympathizers of the trade unions would dare to express the obvious truth which a courageous woman from within the British labour movement frankly stated, namely, that "it is in fact the business of a Union to be anti-social; the members would have a just grievance if their officials and committees ceased to put sectional interests first" (Barbara Wootton, *Freedom under Planning* (London, 1945), p. 97)' (p. 505).

enough to cover the relations between workmen and masters and the regulation of trade or business, did not extend to political or indeed any other objects, and to this extent the well-known doctrine of *ultra vires* was applicable.

The difficulty that trade unions were not constituted by statute (though some of them had been legalised thereby while others did not need statutory protection as being substantially innocent at common law because their dominant purpose was not in restraint of trade) did not seem to trouble their Lordships. Indeed, by a remarkable paradox the union in question had previously been declared in 1911 in the Court of Appeal to be a society *lawful* at common law, and therefore in no need of that statutory legalisation on which the House of Lords relied!

A further complication arose from a conflict of view of the Law Lords: two seemed to confine their judgment to trade unions which were registered, while Lord Halsbury thought that unregistered unions would be similarly affected. In fact registration is optional and it had no effect before 1913 beyond requiring an unregistered union to sue or be sued in a representative action rather than in its unregistered name. In Scotland Lord Skerrington seemed also to limit the *ultra vires* doctrine to registered unions, but if any principle is to be derived from the Osborne Case, it would certainly appear that Lord Halsbury was right. If legalisation be the test, it applies to unions substantially in restraint of trade, whether registered or not. How far Professor Hayek would regard this decision as an undue restriction or as sociologically correct it is not easy to say; his view would largely be determined by political, economic and sociological considerations with which I am not concerned. Certainly it is a curious fact that the earliest unions seeking to enforce minimum wage statutes, were, in a sense, political, and in seeking enforcement travelled far beyond what is now known as collective bargaining.

In 1913, while the restriction on political activities and other objects outside the ambit of the definition in the 1871 Act was removed with certain conditions governing the right of a trade unionist to 'contract out' of political obligations, the fundamental reasoning in the Osborne Case remained. To this day it is by no means certain how far a trade union, lawful at common law, comes within the decision in that case. It would appear, however, that the 1913 Act, by reason of its generality, places unions lawful at common law and unregistered unions in the same category as registered unions. The case of the union lawful at common law, to which I have referred, was never noticed during the parliamentary debates on the 1913 Act and, so far as I know, has escaped comment ever since.

The General Strike and the 1927 Act

The large cessation of labour in 1926 and the subsequent legislation of the Trade Disputes Act 1927 called into question not so much the position of the trade union as such, but rather the proper limitations to be placed on the right of concerted strikes in circumstances affecting society as a whole.

The argument of Sir John Simon (as he then was), that the officials ordering the so-called 'general' strike were civilly liable for damages, raised the problem how far the Trade Disputes Act 1906 could be used by them as a defence. It will be recalled that the procurement of breaches of contract (and in this case there were very many) are protected if made *only* in furtherance of a trade dispute. It was contended by Sir John that in so far as the strike was called to put pressure on the Government its sole ground was not *merely* to further a trade dispute within the meaning of the 1906 Act. He did not, however (as did Mr. Justice Astbury in an unargued interlocutory case, to restrain action until actual trial, heard at the same time) forget that the Act had been decided by the House of Lords to extend to sympathetic strikes in other industries than the one directly affected. Nor did he maintain that there was a seditious conspiracy, which, arguably, it might have been had it purported to coerce the Government.

Thus the sole issue left was whether the magnitude of the stoppage in itself was a ground for saying that it was something beyond a prohibited trade dispute. The opinion of Sir John raises other difficult considerations, not merely the size of the strike; but the effects of a strike in one essential industry, such as one in electric power stations, might produce effects equally injurious to the public as a general stoppage. Eminent jurists differed in their views on the correctness of Sir John's opinion.

It has been decided in the House of Lords in the case of *Sorrel* v. *Smith* and the Mogul case that to act in the supposed interest of a combination of traders to better themselves, even though it causes injury incidentally to another, is not unlawful. Only if the direct object of the confederacy is injury does an actionable conspiracy arise, and the same principle is applicable in trade union action. It would appear, therefore, that injury to the community without a seditious purpose cannot be a final test, though it was sought to be made so in certain cases by the 1927 Trade Disputes Act. Even there the Statute started with the words 'Whereas doubts have arisen'.

In a case in 1846,* at the time of the Chartist agitation, Erskine, J. went so far as to say that if the object of a strike was only to obtain the Charter and not to coerce the government, it was not in itself illegal. As has been indicated, the Trade Disputes Act of 1906 (the special object of disapproval by Professor Hayek) makes the validity of this decision somewhat academic.

But the fundamental dilemma in terms of freedom remains unsolved. A union may sometimes, in fear of a general stoppage, force an employer to dismiss or refuse to employ a particular man or class of persons such as non-unionists. This may seem tyrannical. Morally, it may be so; but equally if members of a union are not allowed to leave their employment on notice duly given, they also have lost their freedom.

Yet Professor Hayek says

> 'the right to strike, though a normal right, can hardly be regarded as an inalienable right. There are good reasons why in certain employments it should be part of the terms of employment that the worker should renounce this right; i.e., such employment, should involve long-term obligations on the part of the workers and any concerted attempts to break such contracts should be illegal' (p. 269). 'We must also regard as inadmissible methods of coercion all secondary strikes and boycotts which are used not as an instrument of wage bargaining but solely as a means of forcing other workers to fall in with union policies' (p. 275).

Conflicting liberties

There are thus conflicting liberties; the issue can only be decided by legislation, but legislation cannot create, though it may diminish freedom. It is interesting to observe that Parliament in England, while interfering with the rights of capitalists under the Monopolies and Restrictive Practices Acts, has not so far, apart from the defunct Trade Disputes Act 1927, ventured to interfere with the practices, restrictive or otherwise, of trade unions as such.

A further difficulty arises from a juristic angle. Supposing, as was

* *Rex* v. *Cooper*.

the case under the Trade Disputes Act 1927 (now repealed except in Northern Ireland), a man is forbidden in the circumstances there stated to strike, that is to say, he must continue to work if the cessation is of the nature of a strike, there defined as the:

> 'cessation of work by a body of persons employed in any trade or industry acting in combination or a refusal of any number of persons who are or have been so employed to work or accept employment.'

What is the position of the individuals comprising such a body? Obviously, their contracts as such have come to an end. Is the continued employment to be deemed to be continued on the analogy of the notional continuation of an expired tenancy, known in law as an attornement of a tenancy? And, while an individual, as such, was by the 1927 statute expressly allowed lawfully to cease to terminate employment or accept employment, directly he exercises this right 'as one of a body' he may become involved in an illegal strike. But what effect this may have on his legal position, whether he is bound by an implied contract or occupies a new statutory status, is by no means clear.

* * *

Thus by a process of historical accident, trade unions have come to acquire legal rights and powers that are privileges in the sense that they are not allowed to other organisations; which indeed are denied them, and whose trade practices to some extent in the case of commercial combinations (but not those of workmen) are controlled by post-war legislation on monopoly and restrictive practices. On this general judgment of the exceptional legal status of trade unions, the views of Professor Hayek are therefore justified.

Confining our considerations to English law, we see that trade union law, like commercial law, has rested for the last hundred years upon the assumption that the persons concerned are *free contracting parties*; but the increased collectivity of the age, as shown in the Restrictive Practices Act and the abortive Trade Disputes Act 1927, indicate that the legislature today will not hesitate to interfere with what formerly were considered inalienable personal rights in the interests, real or assumed, of the state. In substance, apart from the indemnities of the Trade Disputes Act 1906, the law relating to trade unions has not seriously been modified since 1871. How long it will continue in its present highly artificial condition is uncertain.

JOHN ABRAHAM LINCOLN

Born Cheshire, 1899. 1919–20 on staff of Organising Committee of the International Labour Conference (Washington). 1921–3 Ministry of Labour Intelligence Division. 1923–7 India Office, Industries and Overseas Department and Finance Department. Then a free lance journalist and for two years Political Adviser and Public Relations Consultant to National Conference of Friendly Societies and National Deposit Friendly Society. 1947–9, instigated the Voluntary Social Services Inquiry, was one of the assessors to Lord Beveridge and secretary to the Inquiry. In 1955 he acted for the Amalgamated Society of Engineers and Firemen during the railway strike. He has published *The Strange Case of the Friendly Societies* (1946), 'The Problems of the Friendly Societies' printed in *Evidence for Voluntary Action*, Allen and Unwin, 1948. His latest book, *Trade Unions and Freedom*, is now in preparation.

Part 2: Human Rights in Industry

JOHN A. LINCOLN

1. 'Everyone has the right to freedom of peaceful assembly and association.'
2. 'No-one may be compelled to belong to an association.'

ARTICLE 20, *The Universal Declaration of Human Rights*, United Nations Assembly, Paris, 10th December, 1945.

SIR HENRY SLESSER has shown how the trade unions have come to acquire unique privileges at law. In this essay I consider how we may secure human rights in industry and the voluntary basis of trade unions. These proposals are not motivated by fear of trade union power. I am far more concerned with trade union *weaknesses*, which have been fostered by their privileges. Weakness in the unions, and the misuse of their accrued and acquired power, is the concern of those who wish the unions well. And one must wish them well, for trade unions are essential to a free society and a free society is essential to trade unions.*

Indeed, Professor Hayek's statement that

> 'the present position of the unions cannot last, for they can function only in a market economy which they are doing their best to destroy' (p. 283)

carries a warning not only to the trade unions but also to those who seek to curtail their freedom as voluntary associations protecting the proper interests of their members: bargaining and negotiating the wage levels and working conditions of their membership. The warning is clearly that an extension of state control of wage levels is invited to the extent that the proper activities of trade unions are curtailed.

Privilege

In revealing the real and potential threat of the growing power of

* Mr. B. C. Roberts has put this central point in a different way. 'If the unions are to make a constructive contribution to the future welfare of the nation they must come to terms with the market economy, which is an essential feature of a free society, and not seek to prevent it from working.' *Trade Unions in a Free Society*, Institute of Economic Affairs, 1959, p. 3.

the trade unions to the individual, the economy and the state through their use of coercion, intimidation and direction in the government and administration of their organisations and the conduct of their negotiations, Professor Hayek has emphasised the irony of the truth that 'men become the slaves of the instruments of their freedom'.

There is no doubt of the *existence* of the unusual and substantial privileges that the unions enjoy. The points at issue are

(1) their necessity,
(2) whether they are contrary to the interest of the public, the union and the union members, and
(3) whether their removal would involve hardship.

So long as trade unions behave responsibly their present privileges are unnecessary. As an insurance against liability for irresponsible behaviour in industry they are neither justified nor necessary either on the grounds of public policy or of safeguarding the unions. The position of trade union weakness which justified and motivated the grant of these privileges over fifty years ago is now, in fact, reversed. The retention of trade union privileges today could be justified only if they were coupled with special duties and responsibilities. This the unions would rightly reject, for to accept would convert them into public utilities of labour.*

Their present privileges† are potentially, and occasionally actively, inimical to the interest of the public, the union and the member. The cases before the courts in recent years leave little doubt on this score.

One consistent trend in this century has been the persistent and insistent attack everywhere on privilege and its relinquishment, under

* Supplying labour as a common industrial necessity, subject to fixed rules and regulations, at prices fixed by the government and *not in the open market*; thus returning to the economic and legal relationships of feudalism which are the basis of public utility regulations.

† The privileges of the unions, as Sir Henry Slesser has explained, originate largely from sections 3 and 4 of the 1906 Act. These sections are of important historic interest: they have attracted much criticism even from observers who are well disposed to the unions, for example, from the late Professor William Geldart in 1914, from the late Lord Justice Asquith in 1927, from Mr. (later Lord) Jowitt, and from Mr. A. D. (later Sir Arnold) MacNair and Mr. Hubert Philips, in an appendix to the Liberal Yellow Book, also in 1927. But the origin of the clauses has been obscure. Section 3 was not in the Liberal Government's Bill nor in the Labour Party Bill which the Government largely adopted in its place. It was added to the Bill by an amendment moved by Sir Charles Dilke in language which bears a remarkable resemblance to the wording of a suggestion made in an article in the April 1905 number of the *Economic Review* by Mr. W. H. (now Lord) Beveridge.

pressure, by one group after another, culminating in the abandonment of Crown privilege. The trade unions as the last holders of extensive privilege only invite attack by seeking to maintain their present prerogatives. They should realise the folly of supporting political policies of equality from a position of marked legal, industrial and political privilege, whilst seeking to enforce such egalitarian policies through the power given them by these privileges.

On the position at law two further statements merit close consideration. First, Lord Denning, Lord of Appeal, commenting on the rights of the trade union member in 1952, said:

> 'The man is supposed to have contracted to give them (the trade union) these great powers, but in practice he has no choice in the matter. If he is to engage in the trade, he has to submit to the rules promulgated by the Committee . . . A man's right to work is just as important to him as, if not more important than, his rights of property. The courts intervene every day to protect rights of property. They must also intervene to protect the right to work.'*

Similarly he wrote several years later:

> 'the law is inadequate to protect a man's right to work . . . where the law falls short is that it puts too much emphasis on the supposed contract between a man and his union and too little emphasis on his right to work.'†

Mr. George Woodcock, now General Secretary of the T.U.C., has noted the 'particular significance and importance' of the courts' changed attitude to the trade unions, and said that this might be due

> 'to a belief that trade unions have been going long enough to know when they ought to seek professional advice and are wealthy enough to pay for it when they need it. It may be the courts have noticed a spread of the practice of insisting that all workmen in a factory or doing a particular class of work shall be members of the union and have therefore decided that a time has come when a workman's right to be in the union and his rights inside the union need to be carefully safeguarded by an impartial and authoritative body.'

He added that the changed attitude of the courts 'clearly reflects the change in the attitude of the general public'.‡

* *Lee* v. *Showmen's Guild* (1952), 2 Q.B. 329.
† *The Road to Justice*, 1955, pp. 102–3.
‡ 'The Trade Unions and Public Opinion', *The Listener*, 23rd July, 1959.

Since 1950 thirteen cases* involving trade unions have come before the courts – plus the E.T.U. case that is still under hearing. In view of the unions' relatively small area of legal liability, the number of cases is surprisingly high.

In seven cases, *Lee v. Showmen's Guild* (1952), *Bonsor v. Musicians' Union* (1954), *Baker v. Jones* (1954), *Harkness v. E.T.U.* (1957), *Clark v. N.U.F.T.O.* (1957), *Shore v. A.E.U.* (1959), and *Payne v. E.T.U.* (1960), the issue was the wrongful expulsion of the union member. The case of *Spring v. N.A.S.D.S.* (1956) concerned the wrongful expulsion of a member by the union in compliance with the Bridlington Agreement.

The remaining cases raised various issues: *Birch v N.U.R.* (1950), the political fund; *Abbot v. Sullivan* (1952), unlawful dismissal; *O'Reilly v. Musicians' Union* (1955), imposition of a discriminatory levy; *Huntley v Thornton* (1957), conspiracy against a union member; and *Rookes v Barnard* (1961), conspiring by unlawful means. In this last case the defendants, union officials, unsuccessfully sought the protection of Section 3 of the 1906 Trade Disputes Act.

Human rights

In considering the right of the trade union member to work and the attitude of the courts to the arbitrary exercise of trade union power, we are brought to the heart of the issue – the problem of safeguarding human rights in industry. As Professor Hayek says:

> 'the problem of labour unions cannot be satisfactorily solved by *ad hoc* decisions on particular questions but only by the consistent application of a principle that is uniformly adhered to in all fields. There is only one such principle that can preserve a free society: namely, the strict prevention of all coercion except in the enforcement of general abstract rules equally applicable to all' (p. 284).

Rights may or may not be embodied in law, but they are naturally associated with the law in men's minds; justifiably so, for rights are the legislation of experience, and their value lies in their inviolable claim to immunity from constraint by force. Invariably we find that

* For notes on them see Lord Denning, *The Changing Law*, 1953 and *The Road to Justice*, 1955, both Stevens; Horatio Vester and Anthony Gardner, *Trade Unions and the Law*, Methuen, 1955; C. Grunfeld, *Trade Unions and the Individual*, Fabian Research Pamphlet 193, 1957; and B. C. Roberts, *Trade Union Government and Administration in Great Britain*, G. Bell & Sons, 1956, Ch. I. For *Rookes v Barnard* (1961), see J. P. Eddy, Q.C., 'When Trade Disputes Act is No Defence', *Birmingham Post*, 20th May, 1961.

constraints of right that have meaning are constraints of law. Rights have counter-rights; in general, it takes a right to make a right, for the creation of one right establishes another: the right to join a union and the right not to; the right to strike and the right not to; the public right and the private right. It is not illogical therefore to look upon the law as the custodian of rights and upon justice as the arbiter. In spite of the acknowledged difficulties of creating rights in law, I believe the solution may be found by giving rights the sanction of the law.

The legal recognition of human rights in industry would do much to meet Professor Hayek's requirements for freer and more equal conditions in industry and towards bringing industrial associations (trade unions and others)* within the law.

The basic human rights in industry that need to be legally established are:

1. The right to work
2. The right to status and contract
3. The right of association
4. The right of negotiation
5. The freedom to exercise these rights within the law without constraint.

These rights accord with those fought for, and in a large measure secured, by the trade unions, the only difference being in the emphasis placed on the individual. In fact, the status of the worker is based on law, and the status of the unions is secured by the enhanced rights and status of their members. Few trade unionists would assert that a Charter of Human Rights in Industry was not, in essence, a trade union charter. The unions would certainly regard themselves as its progenitors and its future guardian. That is undoubtedly their role by right.

Rules and rights

What changes would a Charter of Human Rights in Industry entail

* 'It would further appear that nearly all trade associations are trade unions, having for their principal object the "imposing of restrictions of the conduct of trade or business" (Trade Union Act, 1913)—and are mostly in restraint of trade . . . As trade unions, they are immune from actions for tort, and, in restraint of trade, they cannot be sued by their members for benefits under the rules nor for any breach of agreement concerning the conditions under which they transact business (Trade Union Act, 1871, s.4)'. 'Trade Associations and the Law', by the Rt. Hon. Sir Henry Slesser, *The Times,* 7th February, 1955.

in trade union policy and practices and in the laws relating to trade unions and industry? It would certainly necessitate revision of many trade union rule books. In the unions the Charter would be made effective through basic model rules* which would be included by statute in trade union rules. Existing rules would be examined by the Chief Registrar of Friendly Societies and those in conflict with the objects of the model rules would be rescinded.

The trade union rule book, considered in law to be the contract between the union and the member, has been allowed almost unlimited freedom. Such freedom is dangerous where there is a suspicion of compulsion in the acceptance of the contract (i.e. the rules)

> 'Both the Chief Registrar of Friendly Societies and the T.U.C. are widely, but wrongly, believed to be effective guardians of trade union conduct. The Chief Registrar's powers, apart from the Political Fund, are virtually nil and his limitations are clearly stated in the *Guide Book of the Registry of Friendly Societies* in the following sections:—
>
> 1,449.—But in no circumstances can the interposition of the Registrar be invoked to direct the holding of a special meeting or an inspection of affairs, or to dissolve the trade union.
>
> 1,435.—There is no power to suspend the registry of a trade union.
>
> 1,359.—But the certificate (of registry) affords no clear proof that the rules of the society are valid.
>
> 1,352.—Model rules for trade unions are not issued by the Chief Registrar.'†

It should certainly be made within the powers and the duties of the Chief Registrar of Friendly Societies to ensure that union rules:

(1) conform to human rights and 'natural justice';
(2) limit judgments and penalties so that they accord with the nature of the breach of rule and with the damage sustained by the union;
(3) provide that charges of breach of rule are considered by special referees and not in open meeting;
(4) contain proper instructions regarding the submission of evidence and providing the member with particulars of charge and evidence;

* Much as the Companies Acts and the Friendly Societies Act lay down model rules which must be observed.

† From my letter to *The Times*, 4th March, 1960.

(5) require that findings and grounds for findings are recorded and made available to the member;
(6) give right to appeal to the union executive council and of final appeal to an independent tribunal appointed by, and presided over by, the Chief Registrar of Friendly Societies;
(7) provide that no decision will become effective whilst it is subject to appeal or under notice of appeal;
(8) acknowledge the Chief Registrar's right and duty to check the validity of all rules;
(9) limit the size of union branches to the accommodation available (at present there are union branches with a membership from 5,000 to 25,000. Any representative democratic business meeting of such branches is impossible.)

The Registrar would be responsible for investigating and adjudicating on complaints of breach of rules or of misinterpretation or misapplication of rules. Changes in trade union practice are more likely to be necessary than changes in policy; the exception is the 'closed shop' and compulsory unionism, but even these practices are not always the result of union policy.

Effects on general rights, trade union practice and law

Each of the five human rights if made effective in industry would mean a change in (a) general conditions (b) trade union practice and (c) the law relating to trade unions and industrial relations. Briefly, under each head these changes would be:

(1) *The right to work*

General change. Strikes called in protest against the employment of a particular person – or to enforce either a union or a 'closed shop' – would be illegal.

Trade union change. Legislation would limit trade union intervention to the duty of the union, in the case of particular trades or crafts requiring special skills and proficiency, to ascertain and certify that the worker was a craftsman or tradesman, possessed of the required skills, and to check that he was employed at wage rates and under working conditions that were not below the level negotiated by the union. Union membership could not be made a condition of employment, and loss of trade union membership could not be a ground for dismissal or for non-employment. This would involve creating a special relationship between the union and the non-member (see below).

Changes in law. It would be necessary to declare that making either trade union membership or non-membership a condition of employment was illegal and therefore no longer a permissible ground for strike action, or for an industrial dispute. Trade unions, employers and individuals would alike be made liable for infringements of the new legislation.

(2) *The right to status and contract*

General change. The main change would be the conversion of the (by now traditional) collective agreement into a contract and the emphasis on the legality and status of the worker, whose contract would be direct instead of implied. Every phase of wages and working conditions – including working rules, redundancy payments, holidays, etc. – would be brought within the scope of negotiation. The change could be secured by establishing the collective agreement between the trade union and the employer's organisation as an agreement of terms of contract, which they would incorporate into a contract of service. The agreement and the contract embodying its terms would be registered with the Industrial Court and the Court would require a return to be made of the number of individual contracts entered into by each employer with his employees. In respect of these registered contracts the Court would be given mandatory powers, and their findings and awards would be enforceable.

Trade union changes. The emphasis would be on the union's role in negotiation and the extended field of negotiation. The change in the collective agreement would *not* affect the status of the union, though its conversion to a contract would bring status to the member. The procedure of conversion to contract would permit variations of working rules and conditions, to meet special circumstances in particular undertakings, to be negotiated locally and added to the contract as agreed schedules. This would remove the grounds of many unofficial strikes which arise frequently from the difficulty of applying a general agreement to a particular undertaking.

Changes in law. Amendment of the Industrial Courts Act would be necessary to establish a Registry and Registrar of Industrial

Contracts and to give the Court mandatory powers. Sections 3 and 4 of the Trade Disputes Act, 1906, would be amended accordingly.

(3) *The right of association*

General change. No change would be involved in the permissive rights of association. The voluntary nature of association would be asserted and preserved. Powers of compulsory membership would be reserved to specially authorised trade unions which have established that compulsory membership is in the interest of the public and the worker. These 'authorised unions' would have to comply with special rules safeguarding their government and administration.

Trade union change. The right of association would mean recognising the voluntary basis of trade union membership. It would also involve the acceptance of competition for members by some of the unions. But it should not imply the recognition, or legalising, of trade union secession or of 'break-away' unions which are in the main unconstitutional and make healthy trade union government impossible. In the changed conditions, however, the pressures within the unions which bring about secession groups and breakaway elements would be unlikely to build up.*

Prohibition of the 'closed shop' and compulsory unionism would not seriously weaken the unions. Compulsion is never applied by a union until an effective membership of 50 per cent of the workers in the industry or undertaking has been secured. This position of power has to be achieved without compulsory membership, which no union dare attempt in its early growth. The fact that such union strength can be obtained by normal growth and development makes nonsense of the claim that compulsion must be retained to maintain union power. The fatal weakness in the claim for the 'closed shop' and 100 per cent trade unionism is that they can be enforced only when the position and strength of the union no longer requires, or justifies, the demand.

The new legislation would lead unions themselves to remove obstacles to trade union development. Under the changing conditions and pressures of the phases of the industrial revolution that we have passed through so far, three distinct forms of trade unions have evolved – the craft, the general and the industrial unions.

* See Dr. Shirley W. Lerner, *Breakaway Unions and the Small Trade Union*, Allen and Unwin, 1961.

Although the craft unions are in danger of becoming a differential in a world of indifference they remain and, in company with the general and the industrial unions, are included in the affiliated unions comprising the T.U.C. Unfortunately the trade unions appear to believe that the industrial revolution is complete and that the evolution of new forms of unionism is at an end. Their concern now is with 'take-overs' or amalgamations, and not with further industrial expansion. Their restrictive agreements make the emergence of new unions almost impossible. Sitting on the Bridlington Agreement,* the unions vainly urge the waves of change to recede. Already the problems created by the awareness of 'white-collar' workers and new technicians in industry, of their power and increasing status, are troubling the T.U.C. General Council.

There remain also 'under-developed territories' of trade unions, for (powerful though they are) only half the weekly-wage workers are in their membership, and women workers, especially those in industries covered by Trade Boards and Wages Councils, present problems to the unions.

The right of association should not only open the doors of the unions; it should equally open their minds. But it would be misleading to pretend that it will not increase their problems. That is unavoidable whilst the union's primary objective is representation and their main activity is government.

Changes in law. The permissive rights of association in the Trade Union Acts 1871, 1875 and 1906 would need reinforcing with penalties for either obstructing or enforcing association.

4. *The right of negotiation*

General change. The range of negotiations would be extended and the likelihood of long-term contracts with escalator clauses to adjust the contract to changes in prices, productivity and profits would be increased.

Trade union change. The union would be required to sign the agreement and the member to sign the contract. This would secure

* *Bridlington Agreement.* The agreement was designed to secure joint working agreements between unions dealing with: (*a*) spheres of influence; (*b*) recognition of cards; (*c*) machinery for composing difficulties; (*d*) conditions for transfer of members. This agreement, like others in labour relations, is not legally binding. The courts have held that it does not give unions power to expel members who do not comply with it. (*Andrew* v. *N.U.P.E.*, 1955; and *Spring* v. *N.A.S. & D. Soc.*, 1956.) See *Relationships between Unions*, T.U.C., 4th edition, 1957.

the negotiating rights and status of the smaller unions and would remove certain restrictions on negotiations which at present operate against the smaller unions and their members. The right to negotiate would recognise the right to strike if negotiations broke down. Strikes against the employment of a particular person or for trade union recognition (approximately 27 per cent of reported strikes) would, however, be both illegal and unnecessary.

Changes in law. Legislation would be required to establish statutory negotiating rights and to lay down the percentage of members employed (in the industry or the undertaking) required to qualify the union for negotiation status.

(5) *Freedom from compulsion (rights without constraint)*

General change. Penalties would be imposed on those curtailing or interfering with the proper exercise of these rights. The result would be a more general regard for right and less for might.

Trade union change. Absence of constraint would certainly mean limiting the number of pickets to three persons to a worker. It should certainly exclude and prohibit pickets from all activity in the vicinity of his home. This intrusion into a citizen's privacy seems difficult to relate to security of employment, individual liberty, and the rule of common law. Picketing should not embroil a worker's wife and family and their peace of mind. (Children will probably be minors at law and should be entitled to protection.) The practice or taboo of sending men to 'Coventry' would be illegal; it would be prohibited in the union model rules and contraventions would be susceptible to publicity and punishment.

The members' sickness benefit and pension payments can be a form of economic constraint. These funds should be treated in the same way as Friendly Society funds. This would give security to both the member and the funds. There is much to be said for carrying out these functions of the union separately as a registered Friendly Society. It would secure that loss of union membership, or threat of loss, would not affect entitlement to pension or benefits or entail withdrawal from the contributory schemes or funds. The involvement of welfare and pension and similar benefits with union membership disciplines is undesirable. Differentiation between Friendly Society funds and benefit should also be removed, for the trade union member is entitled to the same security and safeguard for his funds and welfare membership as that provided by statute for the Friendly Society member.

Changes in law. Amendment of the Trade Disputes Act, 1906, Sections 1 and 2. Existing immunities would be removed. Friendly Societies Act would be amended to include union sickness and similar funds.

Trade unions and the non-member

The abolition of compulsory trade union membership would raise immediately in acute form the problem of what to do about the non-member. The problem has been made difficult, almost intractable, by the way in which unions have reduced it to a claim for compulsory membership. The unions claim, *and rightly*, that the non-union worker enjoys the wages and working conditions secured by the efforts and contributions of their members. Equally, with right, they claim that the non-member is not entitled to enjoy those benefits for nothing. Their reasoning is at fault, however, when they claim that the non-member is solely bound to discharge his indebtedness by taking up membership. This is the easy solution. But, rightly or wrongly, men do not always choose the easy path, and the reasons for non-membership are not readily discernible. Certainly meanness is hardly likely to figure largely as a predisposing factor, for it requires considerable conviction and courage to withstand the pressure brought to bear on the non-member, and few workers would be prepared to endure this for the sake of saving a pound or so a year.

It is more likely that the real loss to the union lies not in the subscription that they would lose, but in their failure to secure the allegiance of a man who has given evidence of courage and integrity.

The problem admits of solution if we state it correctly. First, the union confers benefits on the non-member; second, he is not entitled to them for nothing; third, he should, therefore, pay for them. Given that the worker has contractual status, and the union negotiates the terms of contract, the union *member* is entitled to that service, and his contract, free of charge from his union, because he maintains the union for that purpose. The *non-member* should, on signature and exchange of his contract, pay *to his employer*, the fee fixed by the Registrar of Industrial Contracts which should not be less than the annual contribution of a full member of the union. This fee would be paid to the union accepted as appropriate to the trade or employment of the worker, and the receipt for the fee would be sent by the union to the Registrar. This means some trouble, but far less than that caused by disputes about non-union workers. There are in fact not many non-unionists, and there would be fewer if trade union membership was a privilege and not an obligation.

Rights and responsibilities

The establishment of the contractual status of the worker would bring a much needed element of responsibility and stability into industry. It would secure for the trade union and the member a legal status and responsibility but it would not interfere with either the role or functions of the unions or alter the relationship between the union and the member except in so far as it would renew or restore the original basis of their relations – namely voluntary association.

In comparison with the present position of privilege and (usurped) powers of compulsion, the change offers the unions opportunities for renewed development and evolution. But if the trade unions are to release the potential dynamic of voluntary action they will have to shoulder the responsibility of securing participation. Voluntary association without any real participation by members is a dead duck. To fill the vacuum (created by inertia among the membership) with the collective padding of 'block votes' merely adds to social, political and economic confusion and frustration. It is true, however cruel, to say that there is more life and meaning in the tombstones of the trade unionists of the 1890's and early 1900's than in all the 'block votes' of today, which are power forgeries dangerous to democracy.

Politically the British unions would do well to abandon their peculiar privilege of assuming that all union members are Socialists unless they 'contract out' of the financial levy for political affiliation and support of Labour in politics. They would be well advised if they wish to remain democratic to support and encourage any politically able member irrespective of his party politics. But in a voluntary association it is usual for the members to initiate or propose some political activities or other. It is, however, neither usual nor defensible to assume any person's acquiescence in political participation, whether he is a trade unionist or not; and to assume this *unless* he resorts to a public and identifiable disclaimer adds insult to injury. Imagine the uproar in the unions if every trade unionist was assumed to be, say, Church of England unless he 'contracted out'; or indeed, if he or she were assumed to be Conservative, Liberal, or Communist.

It may justifiably be doubted whether trade unionists can afford a political fund when their ordinary subscriptions do not cover the administrative costs of the union despite their failure to pay their most responsible leaders and officials 'the rate for the job'.*

The relations of the worker with his employer and with his fellow workers are fundamentally man to man, and like most human relationships are best achieved by those concerned without undue outside interference. To accept, and to act upon, this view does not in any way imply that these relationships and the groups resulting from them can or should be outside the law. In fact, the assumption is that they will be within it.

Human rights grow to recognition in, and govern, these relationships, making them possible and enduring. A function of law, therefore, is the maintenance of these rights in the whole range of human association. Trade unions cannot, and should not, be excluded from this procedure. Indeed, the unions must recognise that their organisation and power can have no better or more enduring foundation than that given by the voluntary association of free men within the law.

**Finances of Trade Unions—a Survey by the T.U.C.*, 1956; and George Woodcock, 'For Love or Money?' *The Listener*, 20th February, 1958.

E. F. NASH

Born 1904 in London. Educated at City of London School, University College, Oxford, and the University of Chicago. After holding university posts, joined the Ministry of Agriculture and Fisheries as Economist in 1934. Served throughout the war in the Ministry of Food and was later a member of the Food and Agriculture Division of the Control Commission for Germany. Became Professor of Agricultural Economics at Aberystwyth in 1946. His main interest is in questions of agricultural policy, on which he has written widely in articles and papers. A member of the Runciman Committee on Horticultural Marketing, 1955–6. Co-author with E. A. Attwood of *The Agricultural Policies of Britain and Denmark*, 1961. Married, with one son and one daughter.

IX

Agriculture

E. F. NASH

THE present essay differs from the remainder of this book in being concerned with a single industry. Agriculture deserves this distinction because of the strength of the challenge it appears to present to Professor Hayek's thesis. Whether or not he is right in claiming general agreement among sensible people for the view that the problem of agricultural policy now is 'to extricate governments from a system of controls in which they have become entangled and to restore the working of the market' (p. 367), there is hardly a country in the world with completely free markets for agricultural products, and probably no class of products for which the policies generally followed depart more conspicuously from the principles of the free market system. The type and extent of the intervention practised varies widely, but its general prevalence is evidence of a widespread belief that the free market system does not work in agriculture, however successful it may be in other economic sectors, or at least that agricultural policies which violate its principles are in practice politically unavoidable, whatever their economic disadvantages.

The exceptional case?

Agricultural policy is thus a major example of the tendency shown by legislators, in Professor Hayek's phrase (p. 232), towards 'circumventing or disregarding in individual cases a principle which they would often wish to see preserved in general'. We have grown so accustomed to this tendency that we almost cease to notice the inconsistencies and contradictions to which it leads. Although greater freedom of trade between the member countries is one of the primary objectives both of the European Common Market and of the Free Trade Association, no one is surprised that farm products should be excluded from the internal free trade arrangements of both groups, or that in the controversy about the future relationship between these groups it is the problem of removing the differences between the agricultural protective systems of Great Britain and the major continental countries that attracts attention, and not the difficulty of reconciling these systems with the interests of the general public or with those of the agricultural exporting countries of either group.

Some of the arguments by which protectionist measures for the support of agriculture are defended rest on supposed considerations of national or social advantage, such as greater self-sufficiency against external attack or the preservation of the familiar appearance of the countryside and of the social organisation and culture with which existing forms of husbandry are associated. In such cases the purpose of the protective measures is non-economic and their wisdom or expediency cannot be proved or disproved merely by a consideration of their economic effects, though the nature of these effects needs to be understood before it can be determined whether the measures are likely to achieve their purpose and whether the purpose is on balance desirable. In other cases the advantage sought is itself economic, for example the improvement of a country's bargaining position in trade or negotiations with others, or of its balance of international payments, but here again the purpose is not directly that of advancing the prosperity of agriculture itself. It is nevertheless the latter objective which supplies the main motive for policies of state assistance to agriculture even when other arguments are called in to support them. What makes the case plausible is the common belief that agriculture tends, under free market conditions, to be less prosperous than most other industries in progressive communities and that it lacks the means of remunerating those who seek their livelihood from it at rates which seem reasonable in relation to those obtainable in other occupations. The basic demand is for a more equitable income-distribution between agriculture and other industries than the free market system appears capable of achieving by itself.

But this aim, though it corresponds to a view of the economic functions of the state which inevitably gains acceptance in a society giving equal political rights to all its citizens, is totally unacceptable to Professor Hayek since to him it threatens the very foundations of freedom. He maintains in fact that it is no part of the purpose ot a free society to bring about a distribution of incomes corresponding to any conception of distributive justice, and that policies inspired by this purpose must end by destroying freedom itself. 'Distributive justice requires an allocation of all resources by a central authority; it requires that people be told what to do and what ends to serve.' The ultimate result of the effort to achieve it will necessarily be 'not a modification of the existing order but its complete abandonment and its replacement by an altogether different system – the command economy' (p. 232). So far as the farmer is concerned the methods by which current policy seeks to serve his interests in fact threaten 'to turn him into the most regimented and supervised of all producers'. For government controls of prices 'can be made effective only if combined with direct controls of production' and if they are to benefit farmers 'they must be supplemented in one way or another by decisions of authority as to who is to produce, how much, and what'. Few developments give

> 'so much cause for doubt concerning the ability of democratic government to act rationally or to pursue any intelligent designs. . . . We have reached a state of affairs in agriculture where almost everywhere the more thoughtful specialists no longer ask what would be a rational policy to pursue but only which of the courses that seem politically feasible would do the least harm. . . . Agricultural policy in most Western countries has been dominated by conceptions which are not only self-defeating but, if generally applied, would lead to totalitarian control of all economic activity' (pp. 361-2).

To most people these opinions will probably appear extreme, and to some perhaps absurd. British farmers for example are not, on the whole, conscious of being regimented. Some of them indeed object to the activities of marketing boards, which possess exceptional powers of interference with the normal rights of individual producers, and exercise them for purposes which, in ordinary cases, would excite general censure, if not legal prohibition, as restrictive practices. But the majority would probably not agree with Professor Hayek that

> 'in Great Britain a degree of supervision and control of most farming activities has been established that is not equalled this side of the iron curtain' (p. 363).*

With one or two exceptions the British farmer remains free to produce what he likes, and Professor Hayek's vision of a farming industry

* The disciplinary clauses of the Agriculture Act of 1947, to which this sentence no doubt refers, were in fact repealed in 1958.

whose productive capacity so grossly exceeds the requirements of its market that output must be controlled by authoritative direction may seem to have little relevance in a country which still imports nearly half its food.

These criticisms are indeed more pertinent to the situation in the United States, where acreage allotments have operated for a number of years in respect of certain products. It is of course true that policies of support for agriculture normally increase the monetary incentive to production, and in importing countries the resulting enlargement of the home output is often regarded as the main justification for such policies; but the primary effect of the enlargement is a reduction in imports, and only if the policy is carried to an extreme does the threat of surplus production become sufficiently real to make the quantitative control of output a possible expedient. Nevertheless this threat is not so remote in the United Kingdom that it can safely be ignored in the case of products such as milk* and eggs, to say nothing of sugar beet, where the acreage is already limited in effect by the need for a factory contract, or potatoes, where planting in excess of the quota incurs a monetary penalty. But even if these consequences are avoided we are not necessarily entitled to acquit British policy on other and less spectacular counts of the indictment that Professor Hayek might have brought against it. If we consider what its effects have been and whether its results have been worth their cost, we are still obliged to reach conclusions that are substantially in agreement with Professor Hayek's main argument.

The basic economic problem

What foundation is there for the common belief that agriculture tends, unless financially assisted by the state, to underpay its personnel by comparison with customary earnings in the industrial and commercial sectors of progressive communities? If this is true, how is it to be explained?

This is not the place for a review of the statistical evidence, but we may quote some conclusions from the F.A.O. publication *Agriculture in the World Economy*.†

* As this essay goes to press it has been officially announced that consideration is now to be given to the use of a quota system for determining payments to milk producers. (*Annual Review and Determination of Guarantees*, 1961, Cmnd. 1311, pp. 6–7.)

† F.A.O., Rome, 1957, pp. 53–4.

'Almost nowhere do farmers receive a share of the national income proportionate to their numbers; that is the average farmer generally earns less than his fellow citizens in other occupations. . . It is often argued that farmers cannot expect to receive the same incomes as workers in the cities. It costs less to live on farms, it is said; those who live in the country have certain intangible advantages denied to town dwellers; farmers have fewer needs. This argument may hold true to a certain extent. It is also true that it would be very difficult to decide exactly what agriculture's "fair share" should be. It seems, however, safe to say that in most countries agriculture is inadequately rewarded, both from the standpoint of providing buying power for a decent standard of living and from a comparison with that offered as a return for labour, capital and management in other occupations.'

This tendency has been noticed more or less as a commonplace by almost every writer on the economic situation of agriculture. It is not quite invariable: Adam Smith pointed out in the *Wealth of Nations* that in Great Britain the differences between wage and profit levels in town and country were smaller in the second half of the eighteenth century than in the first, and there seems to have been a similar narrowing of the customary gap during the so-called 'golden age' of British farming in the period before 1870. But the gap widened again later, and its existence at most periods and in most countries is sufficiently well-established to make it seem a normal and inherent feature of the working of the free market system.

The facts then are not substantially open to dispute. Nor is it possible to question the explanation given of them by Professor Hayek himself at the beginning of his chapter on Agriculture and Natural Resources. This explanation attributes the characteristic economic situation of agriculture to the interaction of two influences, each necessarily present in a progressive community. The first is the general advance in standards of living or in real incomes per head of population, and the second the advancing technical efficiency and productivity of agriculture itself.

The first tendency means that the buying power of the average income of each occupied person is increasing over time, so that in the second of two years between which such an increase has taken place we should expect, if the relative prices of different goods and services have remained unchanged, to find consumers seeking to buy most goods and services in larger quantities per head than in the first of the two years. But it is improbable that the increased demand will be evenly distributed over all the goods and services purchased, and in particular it is most unlikely that the demand for food per head of the occupied population will have risen in the same ratio as the demand for other things. The demand for food per head is limited by the capacity of the human stomach and its aggregate amount therefore depends more on the number of human stomachs than on the average real income at the disposal of their owners. But the number of stomachs for which each occupied person has to provide, that is, the number of non-earning dependants per occupied person, cannot be increasing as rapidly as his real income when the real income per head of the total population is rising. If this rise is taking place, therefore, the quantity of food which the average occupied person will seek to buy cannot, unless the standard of living and food consumption was very low initially, be expected to increase in the same ratio as his income. This is one of the most certain of all economic generalisations. It does not mean of course that the demand for individual foods of a relatively costly and highly esteemed type such as meat, milk, eggs, fruits and vegetables, may not increase more rapidly than the total income; on the contrary, a tendency for this to happen is also certain unless the average diet is already at a high standard. But these foods will be substituted for others of a cheaper kind such as cereals and potatoes, and on balance there remains an indisputable general tendency for the proportion of income spent on food to diminish as its total buying power rises.

In reaching these conclusions about demand we have assumed the relative prices of different goods and services to have remained unchanged; what will happen to them obviously depends in part on the changes which have simultaneously taken place in their relative supplies. In a self-contained community employing a constant proportion of its labour force in each industry the total supplies of different kinds of output will change in accordance with the change taking place in the average output per occupied person in each industry. This in turn depends on the combined effects of technical improvement and of increased investment in each industry, which are not likely to be uniform throughout all economic sectors; on the other hand there is no reason to suppose that they will, of themselves, vary in exactly the manner required if the changed composition of the community's aggregate output is to correspond with the changed composition of its aggregate demand. In particular it is obvious that if the rate of increase in output per occupied person in the food-producing industries is equal to the average rate in other industries, and if the composition of their output remains unchanged, the total supply of food must increase more rapidly than the total demand for it unless the proportion of the total labour force employed in food production is simultaneously diminishing. If the proportion remains constant, or fails to diminish with sufficient rapidity, there will be a relative over-supply of food, leading to a fall in food prices relative to the prices of other goods and to a similar fall in the incomes received by the food producers relative to the average level of incomes in other industries. Some foods will, of course, fall in price more than others, and farmers will, in consequence, devote more effort to fruit, vegetables and livestock products and less to the cheaper staples. But this is not likely to enable agriculture to retain an unchanged proportion of the total labour force without a reduction in its income level relative to that of other occupations.

The customary disparity between agricultural and non-agricultural incomes is thus simply an indication of a continuous tendency for agriculture to over-supply its market because the transfer of personnel between agriculture and other occupations habitually takes place too slowly. Too slow a rate of transfer results not only in a reduction of agricultural earnings below the level they would otherwise have reached but also in the sacrifice by the community at large of the increased non-agricultural output it would otherwise have been able to consume, and therefore in a wastage of some of the opportunities for increased consumption which economic progress has brought within its reach. To quote once again from the F.A.O. study:

> 'the percent of a country's population engaged in agriculture is usually, though not always, an excellent index of the living standard of its people; the greater the proportion of farm population, the lower the standard of living.'

Wealthy countries can afford to use a large proportion of their labour resources outside agriculture because their agriculture is productive enough to supply their needs with only a small use of labour on the land. Countries with large agricultural populations are usually poor because most of their labour is required for the supply of basic necessities and little remains available for the luxuries and conveniences without which living standards cannot rise much above a subsistence level.

The error of the protectionist solution

The reason why programmes of government assistance to agriculture are nearly always economically harmful therefore is that the relationship between agricultural and non-agricultural incomes is not merely one of the effects produced by the operation of the free market system but is at the same time one of the governing forces required to direct its working. Measures to increase the farmer's income in circumstances such as those just described almost inevitably make it less profitable for farmers to move to other occupations and more profitable for them to remain in production as farmers. The symptoms of economic maladjustment are alleviated at the cost of obstructing its cure. Moreover, since the assistance given rarely takes the form of an unconditional transfer of income but is almost always offered in the form of higher prices for farm products, it calls forth further additions to output which augment the initial excess. Even if we count the lessened disparity of income which may result from such a policy as a social gain, we have to set against it the effects of the obstacles it places in the way of the transfer of resources which is required if the most effective use is to be made of them, and the loss of income due to the sacrifice of potential alternative output of greater value both now and in the future. These losses exist whether or not the employment of the productive resources needlessly retained in agriculture is ultimately restricted by measures which deprive the farmer of his own economic freedom. Either of these consequences is harmful, but it is the first even more than the second which bring policies of state assistance to agriculture into conflict with the principles of the free society, for the loss of income may be substantial even if the loss of economic freedom is wholly avoided.

The terms of trade argument

These conclusions however have been reached on the assumption that the economy is self-contained; we have now to consider how far they remain valid in relation to regions that are linked to others by processes of exchange taking place across national frontiers.

To the farmers of food-importing countries the economic difficulties of agriculture often seem to spring from the competition of imports rather than from the increasing volume of the home output itself, and most of the measures undertaken for the support of agriculture in such countries aim at limiting this competition and replacing imports in some measure by domestic output. A government which has no scruples about the treatment which it gives to imports can often create a substantially enlarged market for home output in this way, whereas in an exporting country measures tending to encourage production raise immediate problems about the use to be made of the additional or surplus supplies. But the replacement of imports by dearer home production is clearly not in itself of general advantage to the country undertaking such a policy, however much it may benefit the producers whose market is thereby enlarged.

In relation to the world economy considered as a whole it is also clear that measures which hinder the transfer of resources within individual countries from uses in which they are less effective to those in which they are more effective in the satisfaction of demand must in general be economically harmful. But the separate interests of individual countries do not necessarily coincide with those of the world as a whole, and it is not necessarily true that changes which are of advantage to the world as a whole will be of benefit to every individual country. Situations may therefore arise in which one country can secure an economic gain for its own citizens by preventing changes which would be of advantage to the rest of the world, or by initiating changes which are to its disadvantage. A protective policy may achieve this result because of the alteration it tends to bring about in the terms on which the protecting country conducts its trade with the rest of the world. A food importing country which reduces its imports by protecting its home agriculture may succeed thereby in lowering the prices it has to pay abroad for imported food; and because the volume of exports required to pay for food imports is likewise reduced there may be less difficulty in finding markets for them and the prices at which they can be sold may be higher. As a result the volume of its food imports tends to fall proportionately less than the volume of the exports which pay for them, and on balance it may gain more from the improvement in its terms of trade than it loses from the substitution of costly home products for cheap imports.

In consequence of these facts it has long been recognised* that the

* E.g. by Edgeworth and Marshall. Emphasis has been laid recently on this aspect of tariff theory in relation to agricultural policy by Professor Austin Robinson (*Economic Journal*, March 1950, *Three Banks Review*, March 1953, and later articles; *Agriculture in the British Economy*, I.C.I. Ltd., 1957. See also *The Economic Position of British Agriculture* by G. Hallett, *Economic Journal*, September 1959, and the accompanying comment by Professor Robinson).

free-trade rule of policy cannot be supported by the argument that free trade is in all circumstances the most advantageous trading system in the interests of each country. But the practical importance of these considerations is limited. Although it is clear that a country's terms of trade must in general be affected by its trading policy, the quantitative measurement of this effect is exceedingly difficult, since the terms of trade are also influenced by many other factors whose separate magnitude it is almost impossible to assess and which are in any case constantly changing. In particular, short-term economic changes such as the phases of the trade cycle bring about associated alterations in the volume and terms of trade between industrial and agricultural countries simply because the prices of agricultural products are more subject to fluctuation than those of manufactured goods; thus, the fact that British terms of trade tend to improve when British exports are depressed and to deteriorate when the export trades revive does not in itself throw any light on the long-term relationship between the two magnitudes.* Moreover the terms on which an industrial country can sell its exports depend as much on their design and technical quality as on their quantity, and are also influenced by many other factors such as the flow of international lending, all of which are left out of account by the static assumptions implicit in the terms of trade argument. This is, in short, a class-room argument which ignores most of the complexities of the real world, and is far too abstract and theoretical to provide an acceptable basis of trading policy.

In any case the considerations on which protectionist countries base their trading policies are in practice much more a matter of political than of economic calculation. Although the optimum rate of tariff protection can be expressed in terms of a theoretical formula it is very difficult to believe that any such formula would in practice be consistently followed, even if the economic magnitudes entering into it could be accurately ascertained. But the theoretical argument does not of course justify unlimited protection: if the calculation is wrong, or is not correctly applied, the loss to the protecting country may well exceed the gain.

So far the matter has been considered only from the point of view of the protecting country, but the objections become overwhelming

* See the criticism by D. J. Morgan and F. W. Paish of the argument of R. L. Marris, 'The Purchasing Power of British Exports' (*Economica*, February 1955, November 1955, February 1956).

as soon as the interests and policies of other countries are taken into account. Protection for the purpose of securing a terms-of-trade advantage is, in effect, an act of economic aggression from which more is lost by the world as a whole than is gained by the country initiating it. It stands on much the same footing as the use of monopoly methods by groups of producers in order to secure higher prices and enlarged profits at the expense of the general public, and is to be condemned for precisely similar reasons. Moreover, the calculations of the protecting country, even if they are correct in the first instance, are always liable to be upset if other countries follow its example. The policy invites retaliation, and if all countries adopt it every country is likely to suffer. This, by itself, is a decisive objection to any rule or policy founded on the terms-of-trade argument.

In any event it is obvious that the rate of protection justified by this argument does not necessarily coincide with that required to correct the income-disparities arising between agriculture and other industries for the reasons we have already examined. The fundamental tendencies causing the supply of agricultural products to outrun the demand for them would still operate even in a world in which every country followed the terms-of-trade principle in determining its policy. At best the principle merely supplies some economic justification for the maintenance by a food-importing country of a rather larger agricultural industry than it would require under free trade: for an agricultural exporting country the argument of course operates against agriculture and in favour of other industries. But even in an importing country its force is weakened by the low mobility which hinders the transfer of resources out of agriculture and is the fundamental cause of the industry's characteristic economic difficulties. For this low mobility normally ensures that even without a protective tariff such a country will already have an agricultural industry which is over-large in comparison with that which would exist if its resources were perfectly mobile.

The balance of payments argument

In spite of these decisive objections, a variant of the argument which lays emphasis on the improvement of the balance of payments is one of the commonest of those currently put forward in favour of agricultural protection in the United Kingdom. Since a continued balance of payments deficit must sooner or later lead either to stringent exchange control or to currency devaluation, an increase in home production which makes devaluation unnecessary may be regarded as a means of preventing the future deterioration of the terms of trade which a reduction in the purchasing power of sterling in terms of other currencies would be likely to involve. In addition, by easing the country's current international financial position it would help to remove the need for measures of credit contraction to protect the exchange and thus facilitate a domestic policy of expansion.

These are essentially short-term arguments concerned with the particular situation in which the United Kingdom has found itself in recent years, of which no detailed consideration can be attempted here. A currency devaluation is clearly a major event which would have widespread and to some extent unpredictable consequences, and measures which make it unnecessary may be preferred as the lesser of two evils even if they themselves are open to objection in other respects. But as a defence of current British agricultural policy the balance of payments argument is unconvincing for a number of reasons. However the causes of the somewhat precarious position of the United Kingdom are diagnosed, it cannot now be ascribed to the high prices or scarcity of oversea food supplies. The explanation had some validity in the immediate post-war period and was commonly held to justify the programme of expansion in home production. But the change in the world food situation is so complete that a reversal rather than a continuance of the British protectionist policy is now called for.

In the current situation the major world agricultural problem is a shortage of markets and not a shortage of supplies, and British policy, like that of other protectionist countries, continually tends to aggravate it. British policy has obviously helped to depress the markets for certain commodities such as dairy products and eggs, and has forced some of the exporting countries, for example Denmark and New Zealand, to dispose of their output at relatively low prices.* But this does not mean that the increase in British home production has been necessary in order to avert a long-term rise in world food prices, or indeed that any large or continued rise in these prices would become probable even if British policy were completely reversed. Moreover British demand is still so large a factor in world markets for agricultural products that it is not clear how far even their

* For an account of some of the effects of British policy see *The Agricultural Policies of Britain and Denmark*, by E. F. Nash and E. A. Attwood, Land Books, 1961.

sterling prices would be raised by a renewed devaluation of the British currency. If past experience is any guide, many of the major food exporting countries (for example Australia, New Zealand and Denmark) would be likely to accompany the devaluation of sterling with a simultaneous devaluation of their own currencies, thus keeping British food import prices relatively stable in terms of sterling, while reducing them in terms of other currencies not sharing in the devaluation.

If balance of payments considerations have in fact played any important part in determining British agricultural policy, then the details of this policy seem to display a singular ignorance of the problem whose solution it is supposed to have assisted. Considerable encouragement, for example, has been given to products which are heavy consumers of imported feeding stuffs. The feeding stuffs, unlike most other items of British food imports, come largely from dollar sources, but the livestock products resulting from their use do not.* The increased home output of these products has therefore served to increase British dollar expenditure, the magnitude of which has often been a major factor in the balance of payments problem as a whole. But the imports replaced by the increased home output both of these and other products, such as wheat, largely come from countries such as Denmark, the Netherlands, Australia and New Zealand, where payments problems do not exist to any important extent and where, in many cases, a reduction in British purchases has a fairly direct effect in reducing sales of British exports. It is true that farmers have been repeatedly exhorted to economise their use of imported feeding stuffs, just as they have also been urged to reduce their costs and to make no further additions to the output of milk. But since the government has continued to pay them handsomely for disregarding its advice it has inevitably created the impression either that it does not mean what it is saying or that it does not know what it is doing.

In reality, the British oversea trade problem is much less concerned with import difficulties than with the disappointing performance of British exports in comparison with those of other industrial countries such as Germany, as is freely admitted by some of those, like Professor Robinson, who have most strongly urged the case for increased agricultural production as a means of meeting it. But the

* See E. F. Nash, 'The Sources of Our Food Supplies', in *Agriculture in the British Economy*, I.C.I. Ltd., 1957; G. Hallett, op.cit., *Economic Journal*, September 1959.

recognition of the nature of the problem only makes the poverty of the suggested solution more obvious. The protection of agriculture in no way facilitates the measures to develop and improve the efficiency of the export trades which must sooner or later be undertaken if the British trading position is not to deteriorate still further. On the contrary it absorbs resources both of capital and manpower which could be better used in more productive sectors of the economy, and diverts attention from problems which are fundamental to the country's economic future in order to encourage the expansion of high-cost home agriculture at the expense of food-exporting countries whose efficiency is far greater.

Costs and efficiency in protected agriculture

That British agricultural protection is injurious to the interests of these countries is beyond question, but even this result might be tolerable or excusable if it could be shown that the protective system would in the long run result in a lowering of costs and an improvement of efficiency in British agriculture itself. Whatever importance we attribute to balance-of-payments or terms-of-trade considerations, or for that matter to the contribution agriculture may be judged capable of making to other national objectives such as defence, it is still clear that these purposes are more effectively fulfilled by an industry which can produce its output cheaply and with a minimum of state assistance than by one whose costs are high and which is heavily dependent on subsidies. Current agricultural policy seems in fact to be based in part on the assumption that protective arrangements can be effectively combined with measures designed to bring about an improvement of economic efficiency and a reduction in the cost of public support. This accounts for the emphasis placed on educational and advisory work among farmers and for the increasing expenditure devoted to grants for re-equipment and for the encouragement of improved farm practices and methods of production.

The economic efficiency of a farming system or of an agricultural industry however is a matter on which there is much confusion of thought. Measurements of efficiency in physical terms, such as yield per acre or per cow or volume of output per person employed, are in this context inconclusive or misleading, for output has no value unless markets exist in which it can be sold. When markets are dominated by the competition of lower-priced imports and by the inelastic nature of the consumer's demand an increase in the physical volume of output per person employed may do nothing at all to improve economic efficiency if the value of the output is simultaneously reduced by the enlargement of its volume. Even if the rate of subsidy per unit of output can be reduced in consequence of a lowering of average costs, the increased volume of output may still prevent any reduction in the total subsidy expenditure. However striking the apparent improvement of its physical efficiency, the industry makes no progress in terms of economic efficiency, and does nothing to reduce its dependence on public support, unless the number of producing units is sufficiently reduced as their average output rises.

Economic efficiency in other words does not depend simply on the technical competence and energy of the farmer, but also on the structure and organisation of the farming industry. The main reason for the economic superiority which new-world agriculture has long possessed over that of Europe is not that the farmers and farmworkers of the new world are more competent than those of Europe but that they have always been more abundantly supplied with land; and a similar circumstance largely explains the economic superiority which British agriculture itself still enjoys over many of its continental competitors. But the improvement of productive techniques and of the instruments of production is constantly enlarging both the volume of output and the area of land for which a single individual can be responsible. In order to turn these developments to its own advantage and keep the remuneration offered to its working personnel in reasonable relationship to that obtainable in other occupations agriculture must ensure that a sufficient enlargement of the area of land per head of its working population accompanies, and further enhances, the increase in their average output due to new techniques and new machines. If it fails to do so, it over-supplies the market and secures an excessive increase in the volume of its output per acre at the sacrifice of an adequate value of output per head of its working population.

If the land system of the United Kingdom could be reorganised so as to re-group a sufficient number of the smaller farms into larger units there is no reason why British agriculture should require the assistance of protective measures in order to compete with imports and to pay farmers and farm workers at rates equal to those realised today. But it is obvious that a protective system under which subsidy payments are calculated mainly by reference to the cost of maintaining the small farmer's income is itself the major obstacle to any reduction in the number of small farms. British agriculture has inherited great advantages over many of its continental rivals in the farm system produced by the enclosures of the eighteenth and nineteenth centuries and a tenure system which has discouraged the fragmentation and subdivision of holdings. To give agriculture the flexibility which will enable its organisation to keep abreast of current technical and economic changes is a debt which every generation owes not only to its own farmers but to their children and grandchildren. But most of the policy innovations which modern ingenuity has introduced not merely ignore these obligations but delay and obstruct the needed adjustments and burden our descendants with the cost of making good our own defaults.

The reorganisation which British agriculture now requires is no doubt costly and difficult, but the main hindrance to its achievement is not the effort required but the absence of any sufficient inducement to carry it out. The magnitude of the changes needed is not a serious obstacle if the motive of private gain can be enlisted in their favour. But the long series of legislative measures and administrative schemes undertaken in respect of agriculture in the United Kingdom since the war includes only a single Act – the Agriculture Act of 1958 – which can be said to contribute in any way to this necessary process; and this Act itself embodies no bold or original provisions for reorganisation but merely repeals the so-called 'disciplinary' clauses of the 1947 Act and partially restores the free market in agricultural rents and tenancies which that Act suppressed. The recent rise in rents, which until 1958 were completely out of relationship with the prices of farm products, and the restoration to the landowner of a limited power of eviction, have now started to exert some pressure towards the economical and productive use of the land from which tenant farmers were previously almost wholly exempted, and have given some incentive to investment and reorganisation where hardly any existed before. This is a modest and belated beginning, but its effects may nevertheless be more far-reaching than those of all the administrative and advisory efforts ostensibly directed towards the improvement of farming efficiency.

A way to restore free markets

What is needed to revitalise British agriculture is not a complicated set of plans worked out by committees of civil servants but a series of policy changes which will throw the industry open to the transforming technique of the take-over bid. Rewards must be allowed to those who undertake the work of reorganisation and the establishment of new types of enterprise, but it is essential that the rewards should be those offered by the free market itself: the industry must operate under the ordinary rules of solvency and under a price system which ceases to misdirect the efforts and energies of producers by distorting the incentives governing their actions. The fatal defect of a protective system is that it conceals from farmers and landowners the information necessary to determine what kinds of output are most valuable and which productive systems are most efficient. The only kind of price system which escapes this defect is that of the free and unprotected market. Payments for productive effort must be made according to the value of the effort and must not be influenced by the desire to alleviate hardships or the conception of a 'just' reward. The relevance of Professor Hayek's basic analysis to this transformation is clear.

These rules should of course be applied generally and not to agriculture alone. Other industries compete with agriculture for the use of resources and this competition can be satisfactorily regulated only in a free market, just as the supply to agriculture of materials and requisites produced by other industries or other countries should take place at competitive prices which are not influenced by protective arrangements operating to the disadvantage of agriculture.

Although agriculture suffers to some extent from handicaps of this kind which would disappear if all industries were required to operate under free trade conditions, there is of course no doubt that the initial economic loss which agriculture would face from a general reversal of the existing protective arrangements would be severe. But in removing the system of price guarantees and re-establishing free market prices the state is by no means debarred from action to assist agriculture in the process of reorganisation or to alleviate the hardships likely to be suffered by individuals in consequence of it. Instead of obstructing the withdrawal of farmers from an industry which cannot adequately reward them, the state should use its financial power to give active encouragement to it in the interests both of those who leave and of those who remain, and it can quite properly take action at the same time to shield the industry from the immediate losses that would result from any large reduction in the value of the existing price guarantees. Payments made for any purposes of this kind will not conflict with free market principles if they find their way directly into the pockets of the individuals receiving them and do not influence the productive decisions of those who remain in agriculture or induce anyone to remain in preference to retiring or finding another occupation.

As I have explained elsewhere,* the simplest method of compensating agriculture for the withdrawal of the protective system would be an unconditional payment to all those at present engaged in farming, or to those of them deemed to be in need of compensation, calculated by reference to the difference between the incomes now earned under the protective system and those capable of being earned under a system of free market prices. An annuity calculated in this way and payable for life to all engaged in farming, but not transferable to their successors, would, in theory at least, make it possible to bring the protective system to an end while fully making good the loss of income to its present beneficiaries. There is no doubt that compensation of this kind is feasible – a scheme with some resemblances to the present proposal has in fact been applied to the cotton industry; and even if it resulted in continuing liabilities for a lengthy transitional period it would be greatly preferable to the indefinite retention of the existing protective system. There is of course much room for the discussion of details, but the energy and ingenuity of officials would be much better employed in working them out, and in devising arrangements to hasten and assist the required reorganisation, than in continuing to administer the present schemes.

As Professor Hayek himself recognises (p. 364), adherence to the general principle of free market prices does not mean that genuine and important problems of agricultural policy do not exist for which the state must inevitably take responsibility. To the two tasks which he assigns to governments in the agricultural field – the improvement of the legal institutions, especially those relating to land, which govern the working of the market, and the provision of information to assist individuals in forming correct judgments on their own economic opportunities and prospects – there are perhaps

* 'Farming with Free Prices', *The Guardian*, 18th August, 1960; *The Agricultural Policies of Britain and Denmark*, pp. 88–9.

others that can be added without infringing the basic principles to which he devotes so much powerful argument. The special economic risks to which agriculture is for various reasons exposed under free market conditions would create a strong case for some form of insurance operated by the state, if the deplorable record of governments in connection with other forms of state insurance did not almost wholly destroy confidence in their ability to observe the vital distinction between insurance benefits and subsidy payments. In addition, the state often has the opportunity, and perhaps in some circumstances the duty, of taking action to assist agriculture in overcoming the costly handicap imposed on it by the immobility of its resources. Many of the most useful measures open to it in this field are negative, taking the form of the removal of unneeded disincentives to desirable changes or the discouragement of developments likely to hinder them such as the transformation of agricultural estates into large numbers of petty properties in separate ownership. But the reorganisation of small farms into larger units will no doubt often be hastened by schemes which allow the use of compulsion in return for appropriate financial compensation and subject to suitable safeguards.

In philosophical terms Professor Hayek is right in arguing that 'just' distribution is neither one of the purposes nor one of the results of the free operation of economic institutions. Yet large and continuing differences between the rewards given to similar groups of people in return for similar efforts, such as those which often exist between the agricultural and non-agricultural populations of the same country, are not in themselves desirable, nor are they inevitable, or at any rate incapable of substantial diminution, in a properly working free market system. The removal of the fundamental causes of the frictions and obstacles to mobility responsible for them is a gradual process, probably more dependent on education, the improvement of communications, the dissipation of prejudices and misunderstandings, the provision of opportunities for acquiring skill in non-agricultural occupations, and the maintenance of healthy development in other economic sectors, than on any action specifically directed to agriculture itself. But it is a process which is necessary in the interests both of agriculture and of free institutions in general, since without it agriculture will continue to look upon itself as an exceptional case to which the free market rules cannot be applied.

Index

ACTON, H. B., 9, 69–84
Acton, Lord, 7, 31, 63
Agriculture, 171–189
  Acts, 188
Agriculture in the World Economy, 174
Amalgamated Society of Railway Servants, 149
Apartheid, 40
Aquinas, 77
Aristotle, 20
Arnold, Matthew, 20
Astbury, Mr Justice, 151

BANK CHARTER ACT, 1844, 87
Bank of England, 97, 98
Bank rate, 94, 98
Bastiat's *Harmonies Économiques*, 70
Benham, Frederic, 9, 13, 101–17
Bentham, Jeremy, and meaning of 'Agenda', 9
  principle of the greatest advantage, 20
Beveridge Report, 120, 128, 137
Braddon, Russell, 11(f)
Brainwashing, 43
Bridlington Agreement, 158, 164
British United Provident Association, 120, 129
Burke, Edmund, 7, 31, 33, 55(f)
Burnett, 140
Burn's *Justice*, 142
Bury, J. B., 19

CALVIN'S GENEVA, 79
Cambridge Journal, 33
Campbell, Lord, 140
Capital gains, 110
  tax, 112
Charter of Human Rights in Industry, 159
Chartist agitation, 152
Christianity, Origin of, 18
Clark, Colin, 111, 126
Classical economists, The, 17, 55
Closed shop, prohibition of, 163
Coercability, 46
Coercion, 34, 37, 52, 71, 83
  concept of, 41
  definition of, 42
Combination Acts, 139–53
Combination Laws Repeal Acts, 141–2
Commodity taxes, *see* Expenditure taxes
Common Market, 171
Conspiracy and Protection of Property Act, 143
Constant, 78
Constitution of Liberty, The, passim
Constitutionalism and liberty, 54, 63–4
Contract, moral advantages of over status, 83
Counter-Revolution of Science, The, 31
Crompton, J., 140
Currency and Banknotes Act, 1954, 97

DEATH DUTIES, 107, 112
Denning, Lord, 157
Dicey, 54, 57, 62
Dirigisme, and totalitarianism, 10
  and the rule of law, 55, 64, 65
Distributive justice, 72, 78–82
Dogmenstreit, 24
Donoughmore Committee, 61
Droit administratif, 62
Dryden, 70

E.T.U., 158
Economica, 9
Economic centralization and rule of law, *see Dirigisme*
Edgeworth, 104
Education, selective, need for, 22
Egalitarianism, 80, 104
Empiricism of Hayek's philosophy, 41
Enlightenment, The, 17, 74
Erskine, J., 152
Esher, Lord, 143
Estate Duty, *see* Death duties
Existentialism, 73
Expenditure Tax, An, 115

F.A.O., 174, 177
Family (children's) allowances, 120, 129
Federal Reserve System, 95
Federalism and Liberty, 54, 63–4
Fisher, Irving, 114
Fogarty, Michael P., 9, 119–37
Free Trade Association, 172
Free-will *v* determinism, problem of, 45
Freedom, definition of, 38, 42
  social benefits of, 48–9
Friendly Societies, 165
  Chief Registrar of, 160
Future of Purchase Tax, The, 115

GLADSTONE, 31
Gold standard, 89, 90, 97
Government expenditure, level of, 90
  reduction of, 111
Grose, J., 142, 146
Guillebaud, C. W., 126

HAGENBUCH, Walter, 126
Halsbury, Lord, 150
Hand, Learned, 59
Harris, Ralph, 13
Hawkin's *Pleas of the Crown*, 142
Hayek, F. A., passim
Hewart, Lord Chief Justice, 61
Hierarchies, coercive and uncoercive, 79–80
Hire purchase restrictions, 96
Holmes, Oliver Wendell, 59
Holt, C. J., 142
Hook, Sidney, 7
Hospital Service Plan, 120
House of Commons, 33
Hume, David, 7, 33, 55(f)
Hutt, W. H., 12
Hutton, Graham, 9, 17–29
Hypnotic suggestion, 43

INCOME TAX, 106–7
Industrial Courts Act, 162
Inflation as a menace to freedom, 88
  causes of, 92–4
Inland Revenue, role of, 127
Insurance, health, 119
  state, 123
  voluntary, 119, 124
International Labour Review, 132
International Monetary Fund, 97

JENNINGS, Sir Ivor, 57, 58
Judicial discretion, problem of, 59

KALDOR, Nicholas, 115
Krushchev, 76

LABOUR PARTY, 122, 132, 167
Laissez faire, 12
Laski, Harold J., 58
Law, administrative, 61–2
  impartiality of, 58–61
  nature of, 56–68
  predictability of, 58–61
  rule of, and case law, 60
Lees, D. S., 127
Lincoln, J. A., 9, 155–68

MACAULAY, 31
Maitland's description of the Star Chamber, 60
Majorities, tyranny of, 21
Market economy, 47, 59
Means tests, 135
Medical care, 120, 122
Mill, J. S., 20
Mill on *Liberty*, 48
Milton, 31, 33(f)
Minimum aggregate sacrifice, 'principle' of, 103
Minorities, tyranny of, 21
Mogul case, 151
Money supply, changes in, 87
Monopolies and Restrictive Practices Act, 152
Monopoly, 37, 47, 66–7
  state, 122–3, 125–7
Moral rules, 77
Morgan, E. Victor, 9, 13
Motor vehicle duties, 107

NASH, E. F. 9, 12, 171–89
National Assistance, 111
National Health Service, 120, 125–7, 129, 133
National Superannuation, 126
New Despotism, The, 61
Nihilism, danger to liberalism of, 77–8

OAKESHOTT, 33
Osborne case, 149–51

PALEY, 55(f)
Parkinson's Law, 26, 120
Peacock, Alan, 111, 126, 137
Peckham Health Centre, 126
Peel, Sir Robert, 87
Pensions, private, 120, 128
  state, 112, 119
Personal wealth tax, 112
  as replacement for tax on investment income, 114
Picketing, mass, 139, 144, 165
Pigou, 104
'Planning' state, 59

Plato, 20
Poor relief, 119, 121
Predictability and ignorance, 74–6
Prest, A. R., 115
Price stability and employment, 89–92
Private property essential to freedom, 71
Profits tax, 107, 114
Progress as a consequence of freedom, 71, 73, 76–8

RADCLIFFE COMMITTEE, 97
Rechtsstaat, 36, 55, 62
Reinsurance, function of, 132
Rent restriction, 65
Resale price maintenance, 116
Responsibility, pragmatic theory of, 45–7
  responsibility-talk, 47
Restraint of trade, doctrine of, 145
Road to Serfdom, The, 31, 37, 53(f), 64, 65
Robbins, Lord, 7, 9, 10, 12
Robinson, Austin, 179(f), 183
Robson, W. A., 58
Rousseau, 40
Rule of law, and coercion, 39
  and freedom, 38, 71
  and redistribution of wealth, 55, 64
  characteristics of, 53
  conception of, 36
  history of, 55
  idea of, 19, 44, 56–67
  organization of, 23, 36
  philosophy of, 33, 34

SAVING, Exemption from tax of, 115
  need for, 109
Shenfield, A. A., 9, 51–67
Sick pay, 120, 130
Siege economy, 10
Simon, Sir John, 151
Skerrington, Lord, 150
Slesser, Sir Henry, 9, 139–53, 155
Smith, Adam, 7, 8, 55(f), 83, 175
Social security Act, 128
  systems of, 119–31
  tax, 133–4
Social services, Reduction of, 111
  role of, 11
Social innovation, 35
  spontaneity, 34
Sorrel v. *Smith*, 151
Southern States and negro rights, 63
'Special deposits' scheme, 95
Spencer, Herbert, 20, 80

Stamp duties, 107, 113, 114
Statute of Apprentices, 149
Statutes of Labourers, 140
Stephen, Mr Justice, 143
Stephens, The, 20
Study of Public Finance, 104
Subliminal advertising, 43
Supreme Court of America, powers of, 63
Surtax, 107, 108–11

T.U.C., 157, 164
  General Council, 164
Taff Vale Case, 147
Tailors and Weavers unions, 149
Tax evasion, 11
  variations, 96
Taxation, progressive, 40, 101, 103, 105
  proportional, 101, 102, 105
  redistributive, 122, 124, 134
  regressive, 101
Technological progress, 92–3
Thebaid, The, 27
Titmuss, R. M., 126
Tocqueville, Alexis de, 7, 20, 31
Trade cycle, 90
Trade Disputes Act, 1906, 143–53, 158, 162, 166
  1927, 144
Trade union, Acts, 140, 164
  coercion, 139, 156
  financing of benefits, 136
  human rights of members, 155–67
  lack of initiative of, 126
  legal status of, 139–53
  power of, 92
  privileges, 155–68
Treasury bills, 95

UNEMPLOYMENT BENEFIT, 120, 122
Unlawful Societies Act, 1799, 148
Utilitarians, Hayek's opinion of, 47

VICO, 19
Voluntary association, 167

WALLICH, Henry C., 10, 65
Watkins, J. W. N., 9, 31–49
Wealth of Nations, The, 8, 83, 175
Welfare state, 25, 88, 137
Western Provident Association, 120
Whig philosophers, 55
Wiles, Peter, 126
Woodcock, George, 157
Wright, Mr Justice, 142